POWER
IN
WEAKNESS

New Hearing for
Gospel Stories
of Healing and
Discipleship

POWER
IN
WEAKNESS

FREDERICK HOUK BORSCH

FORTRESS PRESS   PHILADELPHIA

Excerpts from "East Coker" in FOUR QUARTETS by T. S. Eliot are reprinted by permission of Harcourt Brace Jovanovich, Inc.; copyright 1943 by T. S. Eliot, renewed 1971 by Esme Valerie Eliot.

Biblical quotations, unless otherwise noted, are from the Revised Standard Version of the Bible, copyright 1946, 1952, © 1971, 1973 by the Division of Christian Education of the National Council of the Churches of Christ in the U.S.A. and are used by permission except when the author has made his own translation.

Library of Congress Cataloging in Publication Data

Borsch, Frederick Houk.
Power in weakness.

Includes bibliographical references.
1. Bible stories, English—N.T.   I. Title.
BS2400.B67 1983   226'.06   82–15997
ISBN 0–8006–1703–7

9760K82   Printed in the United States of America   1–1703

CONTENTS

INTRODUCTION

This book begins with a story that is only one verse long. The vignette is typical of a number of short passages in the Gospels. One finds brief summaries of healings or sketchy introductory narratives which lead into teachings of Jesus or controversies with his opponents. In some instances these appear to be stylistic formulations of the evangelists, composed to provide occasion for the dialogue that follows. If the incidents were shaped around reminiscences of healings performed by Jesus, almost every detail has been pruned away.

There are times, however, when it seems that the process has worked the other way around. Some narratives appear to have been broadened and ornamented with the storyteller's art. By comparing different versions of the same story in several of the Gospels, and by studying them to see what forms they may have had in the early traditions of the churches before they became part of the written Gospels, we can observe how narratives sometimes have been expanded or otherwise altered to suit particular settings.

We recognize, then, that the stories as they appear in the Gospels are the remnants and final stages of a long development. They were told and retold in the first Christian communities. Often they were used in preaching and teaching situations as illustrations of Jesus' lordship, or to deal with questions or controversial issues that arose in the early communities. Even though the churches had a strong desire to remember things about Jesus, it was inevitable that the preachers and catechists, whether consciously or unconsciously, would *use* the traditions, tailoring them for different occasions.[1] Even the reaction of the audience had its influence. A warm reception would encourage the lengthening of a narrative and perhaps the addition of other stories. When the response or the situation suggested that the speaker come more quickly to the point, a tale might be summarized.

After some years the stories began to be written down, probably in collections of linked series.[2] In a few more years the evangelists took them over, incorporating and using them as seemed best for the purposes of their Gospels. A comparison of the Gospels indicates that the processes of alteration continued right through this final stage. The evangelists edited the materials, gave them contexts, and provided their own perspectives in order to share and give emphasis to their understandings of Jesus and his message.[3]

It is clear, then, that the New Testament does not offer us anything like verbatim accounts of healings Jesus might have performed. At best the stories come to us third, fourth, and fifth hand. This realization has frequently been welcomed by those who do not perceive healing activities to be central to the gospel, and who may even consider them an embarrassment to the contemporary presentation of Christianity. A number of theologians in the nineteenth and twentieth centuries came to regard it as a blessing that the methods of historical research dealing with the Gospels developed along with scientific understanding of the natural processes of the world.[4] The stories of cures and exorcisms— once so popular with Christians and often used to demonstrate Jesus' power and authority—now needed to be explained rather than told, even explained away. The further the stories were dissociated from Jesus himself, the easier it was to concentrate on his prophetic and teaching roles and to present him as essentially a prophet and ethicist. Perhaps Jesus had healed a few people, but these activities, according to this interpretation, were quite secondary to his real ministry. Most of the healing stories, especially the details that did not fit with the modern world view, could be relegated to a kind of limbo of anonymous community formation. Unlike Jesus (and enlightened present day believers!) these early disciples were still heavily influenced by primitive religious ideas and superstition.

Nor was this simply an attitude found in theological faculties. There is generally a strong underground rapport between theologians and other Christians, although its character is often evident only in succeeding generations. The awareness that the healing stories could be viewed as secondary was also welcomed in pulpits and congregations by what almost seems a conspiracy of silence. Although these worshipers were often less conscious of the changes, their perspectives had altered in ways that made it difficult for them to hear the healing stories as anything other than curious and naive legends. It became less and less necessary to give them credence or even serious mention. There were more important matters to preach about and to reflect upon. The parables and Jesus' ethical pronouncements were the vital core of his ministry.

Yet the healing stories are not secondary to the message of the Gospels. In the Marcan account, for example, which is usually regarded as the first written Gospel, almost half of the narratives of Jesus' public ministry (chaps. 1–10) is devoted to Jesus' acts of power, most of which are stories of exorcism and healing. And the more deeply one probes the traditions by the methods of critical analysis—however hard it is to reach behind individual narratives to the outline of some actual instance of healing—the stronger is the recognition of the primary role of these accounts of healing activities. At the earliest stages that we can reconstruct they are central to the disciples' reminiscenses about Jesus. They are presented as integral to his teaching and to the effect he had on others. They are often the cause of interaction between him and his disciples or his opponents. Jesus seems to have been convinced that through his ministry the power of the kingdom of God was making itself known and the ancient promises of the prophets were beginning to be fulfilled. In response to a question sent from prison by John the Baptist asking whether Jesus was really the prophet of the new age, Jesus is reported to have replied:

> Go and tell John what you hear and see: the blind receive their sight and the lame walk, lepers are cleansed and the deaf hear, and the dead are raised up, and the poor have good news preached to them. And blessed is he who takes no offense at me.
>
> (Matt. 11:4–6; Luke 7:22–23)

This response, which partly because of its oblique character is thought by a number of scholars to reflect Jesus' own words,[5] is a virtual compendium of hopes for the new age which derive from the book of the prophet Isaiah.[6] It is not inappropriate then that Luke's Gospel presents Jesus as taking over other words from this prophet and using them in a kind of inaugural address in the synagogue at Nazareth:

> The Spirit of the Lord is upon me,
> because he has anointed me to preach
> good news to the poor,
> to proclaim release for prisoners and
> recovery of sight for the blind;
> to set at liberty those who are oppressed,
> to proclaim the acceptable year of the Lord.
>
> (Luke 4:18–19)

The acts of healing and the exorcisms of oppressive demons are not, then, added parts of the good news of the kingdom. They are a crucial way in which the kingdom comes—by which the ruling love and justice of God are made known. They are the acts of power of the approaching kingdom, enacted parables of its healing and saving character. It is impossible to make historical sense of what lies behind the Gospels by dismissing this aspect of the tradition or even passing over it lightly. Whether one today believes in healing powers which go beyond scientific and medical explanations is not here the point. It is evident that in his time Jesus was believed to be a healer. Even the most trenchant critics of the gospel traditions—both inside and outside the Christian faith—now agree that behind the stories of cures and exorcisms there stands "a core of historical reality."[7] Hans Küng sums up this realization: "There must have been cures of various types of sickness which were amazing at least to people at that time."[8] The narratives might better be described as stories with historical elements rather than history in story form, but they do bear an important relationship with the ministry of Jesus.

From a historical-critical point of view one of the bits of evidence which is most convincing in this regard derives not from the witness of the disciples but indirectly from Jesus' enemies. The brief story of a dumb man's healing with which this book begins is followed by an accusation that Jesus performed cures by the power of satanic forces—by Beelzebul—rather than by the power of God (Luke 11:15–22; Matt. 12:25–29; Mark 3:22–27). To this charge Jesus, in effect, replies, nonsense. Then Satan's kingdom would be divided against itself and would fall of its own accord. Our immediate concern, however, is not with Jesus' response, but with the allegation—a charge that is found in the traditions behind the first three Gospels and frequently in the Fourth Gospel.[9] In one sense it is an old and recognizable form of argument which we know as "poisoning the well." We recognize it when it is employed against us and may have perpetrated it ourselves a time or two. It is used when all other arguments have failed and people sense that they are coming out on the short end of the debate. Then it is time to question the other person's motives, morals, or ancestry—in this instance by contending that Jesus' power to cast out demonic forces and to heal came from an evil source. We notice that these opponents did not suggest that his reputation as a healer was exaggerated or trumped up. However much difficulty they had in appreciating his healing activities (even to the point of arguing that such evident good was really bad), this line of argument was apparently not open to them. In their time they had to recognize that in association with Jesus' ministry extraordinary things were happening.

It is reasonable, then, to suppose that healing events did take place through Jesus' ministry and to want to look again at the stories told about them. Our way of access to these stories, however, is not an easy one—not if we are hoping for a hearing that will give us a penetrating understanding of and feeling for what the disciples believed. Indeed, some would say that the path is cut off—that there is no way to reach across the erosion caused by two thousand years of cultural change and the rifts opened by seismic shifts in historical consciousness and scientific understanding.[10] All we may reasonably do is assemble what historical and literary-critical data we can in order to better appreciate the original settings of the narratives and, perhaps, also to help us keep a respectful distance from them.

Some of us, however, will not be content. The stories were first told to capture hearts and imaginations as well as to inform. There are ways in which, if we are to understand at all what was happening then, we must make an imaginative effort to be part of the circumstances of those first audiences. But how are we to do this? Making use of pertinent historical and literary information can certainly be of assistance, enabling us better to discern their contexts and the *world* which the first disciples inhabited. We may be reminded, for instance, that the earth was then at the center of what was believed to be a much smaller universe, a world that seemed to be less subject to the rules of cause and effect and far more open to supernatural intervention.[11] We may also be enabled better to see the peoples of the New Testament era as real people with longings, dreams, fears, and wants not wholly different from our own, even as we are being made aware of important differences between our world and theirs.

Inevitably, we will then want to compare and contrast our longings, dreams, fears, and wants and our ways of trying to comprehend the universe and its processes, the how and even the why of life. We would like, if we could, simply to take over the biblical stories and make them our own, but we know that we cannot. Yet we also realize that without some form of direct engagement on our part—without our investing our own sensitivities and concerns—the stories will only be relics from the past, separated from the real sicknesses and needs for wholeness of our lives.

These two ways of approach—through historical-critical study or by direct engagement—often seem incompatible, so much so that there is a strong tendency either to comment upon the stories from a historical perspective but make little other use of them, or else to try to use them without reference to any critical perspective. We may wish that there was some better form of helpful dialectic, but it seems rarely to take place.[12]

This book proposes that it is the stories themselves, not just their content and character but the very form of narrative, that can encourage a dialogue and help to create a bridge between the two worlds of the biblical past and our present. Let me create an analogy: let us say that we have an interest in the people of islands of the South Pacific. Unfortunately our credit card limit is not large enough to make possible a visit. We instead assemble a good deal of data about their sociological, economic, cultural, religious, and demographic circumstances. We believe we have gained some understanding of them, but now we want more. We want some *feel* for their lives. We want to imagine our way into their world to see if we can gain some new perspectives for ourselves. Our way is their stories, and, again, not just the content of the stories, but the vehicle of story itself which allows us to make an imaginative entry.

All of us realize that stories possess a mysterious magic. We use them to help give connectedness and significance to life—to apologize, to explain, to say why we value what we do, to tell ourselves and others who we are. Yet we are not at all sure how the stories relate to what is going on *out there*. We live, after all, in a fleeting present which is related only by memory to the past and by imagination to the future. We cherish the capacity of narrative to establish links and, in a sense, to hold life together. But are we able to do this because there is an essential quality to the structure of universal time and events that is inherently story-shaped? Or is it that our minds are so shaped as to give a story form to life?[13] However we try to understand the relationship, we become aware that what we call *life* seems to be the result of a complex and often cryptic interplay between the world *outside* us and our efforts at interpretation, often through stories together with their metaphors and symbols. The very telling of a story seems to be based on a belief or on some manner of hope that life either has or can be given significance and meaning.

Yet what then is the relationship of story to event? Every story is a kind of intensification—distorting to some degree, leaving out this or that, telescoping, or seeing possible connections only afterward. Some storytellers become bolder, heightening character, transposing, using flashback in order to bring out truths that they believe we might otherwise miss. Certain stories we recognize as being more fictional; others represent more of an effort to report events, but we know that the line between the two often wavers and becomes indistinct. We know how fiction can reveal truth while reportage may disguise matters of great moment.

The Gospel stories of healing were clearly once used to invite hearers to discover what their tellers regarded as of vital significance about life. We have seen that they have a basis in reminiscence, but were often retold and given new contexts to draw out their meanings. Because we, too, live in a world structured and given much of its significance by means of narratives, these stories can provide us with forms of experiencing life through which we may try to discover how much can be shared. Sallie McFague put it this way: "We all love a good story because of the basic narrative quality of human experience; in a sense, any story is about ourselves, and a *good* story is good precisely because it somehow rings true to human life."[14]

We might just read the Gospel stories of healing again, present historical background information and our own commentary, and hope that these stories would thus take on new life for us. For most hearers today, however, some further incitement to imagination would seem helpful if not necessary. Although we can rightly admire the artful economy of many of the Gospel narratives, their brevity provides a problem for modern readers and hearers. Perhaps this would not be so if they recognized that things left in the shadows (the recesses where motivation is hidden from the other and perhaps even from the actor), the gaps, and ambiguities in the narratives are actually invitations to the listeners' imaginations.[15] Good stories both disclose and hide their significances for us. The hiding is meant to lure us into discovering meaning for ourselves. The silences in the text encourage us to speak.

This awareness was obviously vital to the Jewish haggadah or narra-tive expansion of biblical texts. It can also be seen through the artistic imagination of numerous painters, especially prior to the nineteenth century. But the manner in which Scripture is today put on a pedestal tends to severely restrict the recreative imaginations of many people. The words have become so sacralized that, with the exception of a few meditative traditions and approaches from a psychological orienta-tion,[16] it is as though interpretation by imagination were forbidden, with the result that the stories remain closed to many hearers. One interpreter put the larger issue regarding the contemporary hearing of Scripture in these terms:

> The key question in the new hermeneutic, then, is how the New Testament may speak to us *anew*. A literalistic repetition of the text cannot *guarantee* that it will "speak" to the modern hearer. He may understand all of its individual words, and yet fail to understand what is being said.[17]

The problem has been compounded by the emphases laid upon the reading of biblical texts since the rise of historical consciousness in the eighteenth century. The two predominant questions asked of a passage (by both the more liberal and the more conservative interpreters) have been, "Did it happen?" (or, "How did it happen?"), and "What mean-ing can be drawn out of the text?"[18] This is rather like suggesting that the value of *King Lear* could be exhausted by investigating its historical antecedents and then drawing out the message that true love will not advertise itself for its own advantage and may be seen too late. The story would then be retained only to illustrate the major points.

Often lost sight of has been the awareness that truth can be expressed in many ways and that there are significances in stories that can be experienced only by sharing in their telling and hearing. The primary function of a story is not to illustrate or symbolize a meaning, "but rather the meaning is embodied in the form of the story itself."[19] The Gospel stories are not illustrations of what might better be said in propositional form. The stories are the gospel and they express beliefs about life lived in the presence of God which, in an important sense, cannot be articulated in any other manner.

The approach taken by this book to nine New Testament stories cannot deal fully with all of these problems, but our purpose is still ambitious. It is hoped that what follows will initiate and then further dialogue between important historical-critical insights and our contemporary questions and interests. The story—imaginatively entered into—is meant to be our vehicle, our time machine. Our dialogue can then help us so to reflect upon our own circumstances as to spark the telling of new stories and parables of our own. Our interest in the values of the story for the communal settings of liturgy and preaching, for teaching, counseling, pastoral care and for personal devotions will, I trust, become evident.

If one were to be highly methodological as in a classroom, it might seem best to begin each chapter with historical-critical information before proceeding to the story and then contemporary reflection. We would discuss ways in which the story was first understood before thinking about how it might be appreciated in our day. My methods are less formal but, I hope, more suited to the ways in which many of us are prepared to approach the stories and their themes and to our need for a more continuous dialogue between present and past, between our questions and those raised for us by the story. We start with the text. Readers might well voice it aloud and hear the scriptural words again. They may wish to begin to imagine the story for themselves. We then usually proceed to an imaginative retelling of the narrative. Sometimes pertinent historical information is supplied at the beginning or as we go on to help us along the way. We next reflect upon each story from a contemporary perspective, weaving in additional historical and literary understandings. The footnotes give references and provide further material for those who wish to pursue their research. Finally we should go back to the beginning with only the New Testament text before us, now enlightened by new insights and appreciation.

In the conclusion to their study *Miracles in Dispute: A Continuing Debate,* Ernst and Mary-Luise Keller ask,

> How can this religious tradition belonging to the past . . . be taken into and absorbed into the present without contemporary life being restricted by it, yet so that the essential human experiences preserved in it are not lost? That is the leading and still unanswered question which runs through the criticism and interpretation of miracles in modern times.[20]

Our presentations of Gospel healing stories are intended as steps toward answering this question.

The use of the demonic to explain illness in the New Testament provides an example of how this approach may be helpful. Often we seem to be given little choice when it comes to demons and exorcisms in the Bible. We are, on the one hand, to attempt the feat of accepting the reality of demons (as we think first-century people conceived of them) and of bringing them straight into the era of television and computer technology. Our only other choice seems to be to relegate the language about demons to a primitive mythology from a superstitious culture which we are right to ignore from the pulpit and in counseling and spiritual direction.

Through sharing in the Gospel stories, however, we are encouraged to probe at a deeper level. What was it that first-century Christians were experiencing and trying to describe? Is there anything like this in our lives? Although we may give them different names, we too may come to recognize forces that are part of us, yet are seemingly our enemies— aspects of ourselves with power to injure and weaken us but which we can only partly explain. We know how much we too long to be healed of them.[21]

Our ways of retelling the stories will vary. In part this results from an effort to suit our narration to the particular biblical story. But most of the stories could fittingly be told from several different points of view and in different story forms. The primary purpose of the variety is to remind us that we may continue to be inventive and that we are meant to play a number of roles—to obtain at least several perspectives in a full hearing of each story. One of our stories is told twice to emphasize this point as well as for the fun of retelling. The variety is an invitation to readers to imagine their own windows and doors into the narratives.

All along the way risks are run. It is inevitable that our narration will miss some points and slant others. The stories cannot be related without imparting to them our special concerns, emphases, attitudes, and as- sumptions. Some of the historical information will help to provide balance, but we must remind ourselves that every act of interpretation involves such risks.[22] Different translations do this. (I regularly have my classes translate the stories to remind them that all the English versions are retellings.) Even the reading of the passage aloud by different readers offers variant emphases. Every story—in order to be a story— calls for the participation of its readers and hearers. Just as a play only *is* a play when it is enacted and seen by an audience, so a story is only a story when it is entered into, and that participation means some form of re-presentation. Our justification for taking those risks is the awareness that nothing could be more unfaithful to the original purposes of the stories than to fail to try to make them speak anew.

One final caution: This book becomes more difficult and places more theological and personal demands upon the readers as story follows upon story. We begin with a story for which we have already set the context: the single verse that tells of a mute who was enabled to speak. Its brevity allows full play for our imagination. The healing of the paralytic then quickly involves us with questions about the relationship between psychological and physical illness and health, between sin and sickness, forgiveness and salvation. We next relate Zacchaeus's story, an enacted parable of spiritual and emotional healing. It is a paradigmatic tale about the power by which Jesus heals and brings an individual like Zacchaeus to a new way of life. The awesome narrative of Legion, the Gerasene demoniac, haunts us and dramatizes the strength of the forces of evil. It compels us to struggle with questions concerning the demonic and how we might understand the biblical language about evil spirits and exorcisms in the twentieth century. We see how a madman becomes a witness to Jesus.

From among the many New Testament narratives dealing with exorcism, with discipleship, and with Jesus' authority to heal, these stories have been chosen because of their representative character and their capacity both to challenge and to communicate with our contemporary attitudes and concerns. We next tell of the Syrophoenecian woman, a story that shows Jesus breaking through contemporary mores in order to extend the kingdom's healing power. His freedom may be seen as a signal to those who today seek to reach out in new directions. The story of the man with the withered hand forces us to wrestle with the role of the law and what it means to go beyond law in order to heal. Jesus' dialogue with the lawyer and the parable of the good Samaritan involve us still more sharply in the struggle between the new power of the kingdom and those who want only to see themselves as ethical. The parable tells of both a healer and one who was healed.

Then there is Bartimaeus. The religious officials of the time could claim special insights. The disciples had seen Jesus. But it is a blind man who is given the vision that allows him to perceive Jesus to be his Savior and to follow him on the way toward Jerusalem—to passion, crucifixion, and resurrection. He becomes the exemplar for all later disciples. We conclude with Paul's story—the story of Jesus' convert and ardent apostle, who cured others but was not healed of his own disability. The story forces us to probe our own circumstances of discipleship as we try to understand why and how healing does and does not happen.

As we proceed, the questions will become more difficult; the mystery of how God is present in our world will deepen. There will be seeming contradictions and paradoxes. This is not the author's doing. It happens here because this is what happens in the progression of the gospel. Full of opportunity and joy, it still is no easy road. Even the evangelists knew many difficulties in their efforts to interpret Jesus' acts of healing. This soon became true for other early Christian believers and theologians.[23]

The issues and questions become more difficult because the healing stories involve much more than physical healing; they are concerned with salvation. From the beginning there is controversy as Jesus uses the healing acts to point beyond themselves to the consummation of the inbreaking kingdom of God. The controversy foreshadows the cross which shines toward new life. Before long we are caught up in every issue with which the gospel confronts us.

A number of friends have read earlier versions of these chapters and have given me the benefit of their suggestions. I wish to offer particular thanks to Professors Sherman Johnson, Pierson Parker, and James McClendon, to Esther Davis, Barbara Borsch, George Tinker, Robbin Clark, Gary Commins, Maria Wallin, and Susan Buck. I am also grateful to students at several theological seminaries and to participants in at least a half-dozen clergy conferences who listened to these stories and shared in them through their questions and counsel and stories of their own. I happily dedicate this book to my students in the classes of 1973 through 1983 at the Church Divinity School of the Pacific and to my former staff and faculty colleagues there.

1 | A DUMB MAN

Now Jesus was casting out a demon which made a man dumb; and when the demon had gone out, the dumb man spoke.

Luke 11:14 (See Matt. 12:22)

Since he could not speak, he would have been a poor man too. Although he found occasional employment as a fruit picker, most of the year he lived as a scavenger. On some desperate nights hunger made him a petty thief driving him to steal from the neighboring fields or barns.

Nathan had continued to live with his parents well beyond the time a young man would normally have been on his own. After his father drowned, Nathan and his mother became more and more dependent on one another. During the next several years she was the only person he really related to at all.

For the few people who knew Nathan, this was the most poignant aspect of his mother's sudden death. He was now alone in a world to which he could not relate by any normal means of communication. He was unable to share with another human person—to tell why he was crying or laughing. He could not describe how he felt with his mother gone, nor how he felt about the stray dog which followed him home one day.

Life does offer some compensations. Nathan and the dog took long walks in the countryside together. To the people of the nearby town they seemed virtually inseparable. Perhaps a special bond had grown between them, and Nathan may have developed other ways of communing with nature. Still, there was no escaping the fact that Nathan was friendless as far as any human relationships were concerned. Maybe there were compensations, but he had no contact with society, no community, and no stimulation to thought or growth from other people. His mother at least had talked to him, telling him stories of the neighborhood. But now no one took the time. And the circumstances fed on themselves. As Nathan found no companionship, he began more and more to take on the habits of a recluse.

He became unkempt and even slovenly. His beard was ragged. People wondered if he ever changed clothes. He looked as bad as he smelled. He walked about with his head down. If someone did chance to speak to him, he glanced up with what seemed a strange glint in his eyes. This frightened people off, for Nathan had grown into a big, muscular man who, some began to fear, might be crazy. It was weird enough not to speak. Who could tell what thoughts went on in his head, or what he did at night, or with what spirits he might be in league?

During daylight hours, if there was a safe place to run to, the neighborhood children would sometimes make fun of him. "Dummy, dummy," they would shout. They threw rocks at the shack his house had become and laughed when he stood in the doorway and shook his fist at them, opening his mouth while no sound came out. Once or twice some thought he managed to make a kind of strangled moan, although others said it was his dog who actually growled the noise. Finally the children grew bored and went away to other pursuits. What they then could not see was Nathan miserably pounding his fists into his straw bed, tears running down his dirty, bearded cheeks.

After a time there were only a handful of people around who remembered when it had been different. Few recalled that when his parents were alive Nathan did sometimes smile and laugh and even play games with other children, at least games which did not require speaking. But, if any of those children—now grown—remained in the neighborhood, they did not visit Nathan any more. Nathan himself began to appear prematurely old, and most people did not even know or stop to think that he had once been a child too.

Occasionally one parent or another would admonish the children. Yet kids will be kids! Anyway, people began to think, Nathan ought to make some effort himself. In a sense, after all, one gets what one deserves. Just because he could not speak, didn't mean dumb Nathan had to be off by himself so much and dress in such a filthy manner and act so strangely. If he wanted people to treat him differently, then he should do something about himself.

Now and then, if the conversation was really dull, someone might speculate a little about why Nathan was the way he was. The usual answer (because this was the way the people of the time explained strange and otherwise inexplicable phenomena) was that Nathan had a demon. He was possessed by an evil spirit which had somehow come to dwell in his mind and had seized his power of speech. How such a thing could happen was unknown—mysterious. Still, there was likely a reason for it: a sin or evil compact he had made as a very young boy, or something his parents or even one of his grandparents had done. But, you could mark their words; however you tried to explain it, the devil was behind it, and one of his minions controlled Nathan's tongue and kept him dumb.

Nathan himself had heard this explanation—not when people talked about him in their gossip, but again from the children. They mocked him: "He has a demon; he has a demon." One little boy had even come close enough to stare at Nathan and to ask whether he was a demon.

It had set Nathan to wondering. Why, after all, could he not speak? It did seem as if there was something inside of him which he did not understand—a power that was part of him yet alien, that controlled his capacity to communicate and to shape his thoughts into spoken words. It frightened him to think that something strange might live within him, though it was hard to find a better answer. It would help him to understand why others so avoided him.

What he did not understand was why this had happened to him. It was hard to believe that something his parents or grandparents had done would be so cruelly laid on his life. Maybe it was something he had done as a tiny child, though it was impossible for him to remember now. Somehow, somewhere along the line and for reasons he did not understand, he must be guilty of a grievous sin. He was puzzled and confused. Yet at the same time he found himself angry—angry with the people who rejected him, resentful of a world in which he was an outcast and a world which was often so hard to enjoy, and bitter toward whatever kind of God could have made him like this and then left him alone. He wanted to hope it could be different for him, although he had also learned how cruel hope could be.

Some of these thoughts were in his head the day he eased himself into the crowd that had gathered around the one they called the new prophet. The prophet was talking about the new hope and the power of God coming to cast out demons and evil. The noise and the press of people frightened Nathan, but he decided that there were so many strangers no one would take notice of him.

Of course, there had been others before this Jesus. About two years earlier another miracle worker had been through the region, one who said he could expel demons. Maybe he could. Nathan had never found out. He never had enough courage to offer himself for what was called an exorcism.

A few people in the crowd noticed Nathan. Their assumption was that the poor fellow must be bored out of his skull. In any case, he wasn't really dangerous. If he could find a little entertainment in what was taking place, there was no harm in that. At least he was quiet. Others kept shouting out and interrupting what was actually an intriguing argument between this prophet and those who were accusing him of being in league with Satan. It was like a carnival, with Jesus trying to relate stories and tell about his faith that the kingdom of God was already beginning, and others questioning his ideas—while some kept calling on him to perform a miracle and to prove what he said with mighty signs.

What several neighbors now saw, however, did surprise them. Dumb Nathan was no longer hanging around the back of the crowd with that haunted look. He was practically up front, and he appeared to be paying attention. Then two of the local farm boys grabbed Nathan, each by an arm, and brought him right up before Jesus. It was hard to hear, but they said something about this being a man who had had a demon of dumbness all his life. Could the prophet do anything about that?

In the excitement afterward no one could remember exactly what had happened or what was said. Jesus apparently had asked for the man's name and then had spoken to Nathan for a moment before placing his hands on him and performing the exorcism. What seemed incredible, of course, was that Nathan—for the first time anyone could recall— actually spoke in return. Everyone in the crowd who had known about Nathan at all was astounded.

Perhaps no one in that crowd would have ventured to explain how Nathan was enabled to speak. If it was difficult for them, it must seem just about impossible for us. Our whole way of viewing the world has changed. Our understanding of physical and emotional capacities has been altered dramatically.[1] Still, as we hear Nathan's story, we also recognize that there are profound levels of human experience at which we can share aspects of Nathan's condition.

Many of us may know people who are incapable of speech, or nearly so. We may visit elderly people in convalescent hospitals or retirement homes. These are places where one often encounters lonely individuals whose outlooks appear to have shriveled with their bodies. Their lips seem sealed. They speak to no one and no one speaks to them. If we greet them, they may not even look at us. It takes great patience even to awake alertness in their eyes. Such people are relegated to the farthest limbo of society.

I know a man who began to appear from time to time at public functions of the theological seminary where I once taught. In part he seemed attracted to the school because of the newspapers and the library. Maybe he came because other people were there, although for many months he showed no interest in them. He often behaved strangely. There was a haunting aura about him and a warning glare from his eyes should he look up. His lower jaw would move a little menacingly. They said he was on drugs. People would actually back away from him. Some wanted to have him arrested.

He would not speak to me even when I spoke to him. Once or twice I caught him sitting down and sat opposite him and asked a few questions. He would not or could not respond. It was hard not to feel annoyed as well as frustrated, perhaps a little angry. His very presence was a bother and a disturbance. One wished he would just disappear as he had come. Dressed in his ill-fitting and unkempt clothes taken from boxes for cast-offs, he appeared to be making the school furniture dirty just by being there.

Although he seemed from time to time to mumble to himself, I never saw him talk to anyone. I was not able, in my sporadic efforts, even to hold his glance. I began to realize that he was very frightened, though he also had the cunning and daring of a beggar.

I thought once or twice about trying to touch him. For a sick, troubled, or despondent person, a touching hand from a pastor or friend can often be a great gift—even life-saving in a sense.[2] We realize that for someone like Nathan or this man who had appeared at the seminary, or for the elderly in convalescent homes, it may have been a very long time since they were touched by anyone in care and love. They may see themselves as untouchable as well as unlovable. A hand on theirs tells them otherwise. Physical contact establishes a relationship—also when it is a reaching from the sick person to the one wanting to help—through which the power of caring can flow. But I was not able to reach out my hand to him.

Some of the students called him "Shovel-Mouth"—not to his face, mind you, though I suspect he knew that they spoke mockingly of his behavior. They gave him this name because of his propensity for showing up at almost every school function where free food was involved, and sometimes when it was not free. On those occasions he ate with great intensity—huge amounts of food—never speaking or looking at anyone.

I am sure I could have tried harder, but it is not easy to continue after such rebuffs. I could have believed that he was without the power of speech—except that one of the students, by a great effort, had gradually established a form of relationship with him. Eventually she was able to learn his name and something of his background and circumstances. She helped me and others to begin to see the one we knew only as "Shovel-Mouth" as a person.

Encouraged by her example, I tried again. He was shuffling up the street as I was unpacking the back of my car after the Christmas holidays. I do not think he saw me until he was almost even with the car. "Happy New Year, Tom!" I called out. He looked up, surprised. "Yes," he mumbled, "thank you." For a flickering moment I also read some form of genuine communication in his eyes. I cannot even tell for sure what it was, only that it was something I had never seen in him before.

The story of Tom does not have any clear denouement. He still does not easily maintain a conversation, and he continues to have his problems. But he learned to talk again, with me and others. Several students try to see that he receives some decent meals. On good days he can sit and share pleasantly with them. He obviously enjoys talking with children. They come to greet him. No one is afraid.

Many of us know someone like this—if not like Nathan, then like Tom. What would we say about them? Perhaps in some people the speech impediment is so basic—so rooted in some physical fact—that we, at least, may find no grounds to imagine hope for the recovery of speech. But there are other times when we know more about the demons that tie their tongues. We probably would not call them demons though, to be sure, to them it is a power within—part of them, yet also seemingly foreign—that forbids them to speak. In some instances we might know that the inability to speak is the result of emotional trauma—of fear or guilt so great that it prohibits most, if not all, communication. For many of the silent elderly (often falsely labeled senile) one comes to learn of their extreme anxiety about their conditions and their futures, and about a loneliness that winds a constricting circle. (Anxiety derives from a word which means to tighten or strangle, and it is also related to words like anger and anguish.) In many of these circumstances we realize that it will take an extraordinary power to countermand such forces and to free these people from the bondage they experience.

We also grow aware that there are ways in which the story of Nathan is the story of us all. At least at some point in our lives, we too have known the enormous frustration of not being able to speak. Perhaps guilt drives us to the edge of despair. At times the guilt may display its power in forms such as anger and even be so strong as to have to be suppressed, so that we have difficulty recognizing it for what it is. We are incapable of making our apology—to confess ourselves and to begin again. We may be physically unable to speak to certain people or to address particular subjects. Maybe we know members of families who are tragically like this. Sometimes whole communities may find there are issues that they are incapable of discussing.

Or there is fear. We are afraid of people who are different or of ideas that challenge what is fundamental to our perception of ourselves. We seek to avoid and to deny. Some subjects become taboo and we cannot even make jokes about them. We do not converse across certain racial or class or social barriers. "We do not speak of politics or religion here" was the old saying in some clubs or social circles. (Sometimes this taboo may even apply in churches!) In other words, we do not talk of anything that really touches the depths of our lives and our relationships. We address ourselves only to trivia and we speak in banalities. We are afraid to speak straight from our hearts. We cannot say how we truly feel, or tell of our passion and our love. The sense of loneliness and alienation tightens.

Loneliness becomes the evidence of our unacceptability and produces anxiety. Anxiety then drinks its own juices. We are worried that our words, our views, and even our thoughts are of little worth. If people know what we really think and what motivates us—know what we are really like—they will know how worthy we are of rejection. So we must disguise, employing even the words we do speak for camouflage. We must hide ourselves behind a barrage of phrases. In situations where we want to speak from deep within, our anxiety twists our tongues so that we say other than the empathy and forgiveness that are needed. In perplexity and frustration we hear our words or our tone of voice telling something different from what we intended. Or we may not be able to speak at all. Afterwards we shake our heads wondering what is in us.

We hear Nathan's story and we recognize it as a story about people we know. Although we may be fluent in three or four languages, we hear also of ourselves. For we too long to meet the one who will know our name and help us to overcome the impediments in our speech and better communicate with one another. When we do, when our dumbness is driven away, we can again share our stories and tell of our healing and new-found willingness to trust and hope. We find a new language capability—true freedom of speech. We may hear of the advent of the new possibilities of the kingdom of God in the words of Tom and in the words of the elderly woman describing her grandchildren, in the sounds of the family that is able to laugh with one another again, and in the efforts of the community that is conquering prejudice. We may discover too a new capacity to enter into and to tell the Gospel stories of healing and discipleship. "Then shall . . . the tongue of the dumb sing for joy" (Isa. 35:6).

2 | THE PARALYTIC

And when Jesus returned to Capernaum after some days, it was reported that he was at home. And many were gathered together, so that there was no longer room for them, not even about the door; and he was preaching the word to them. And they came, bringing to him a paralytic carried by four men. And when they could not get near him because of the crowd, they removed the roof above him; and when they had made an opening, they let down the pallet on which the paralytic lay. And when Jesus saw their faith, he said to the paralytic, "My son, your sins are forgiven." Now some of the scribes were sitting there, questioning in their hearts, "Why does this man speak thus? It is blasphemy! Who can forgive sins but God alone?" And immediately Jesus, perceiving in his spirit that they thus questioned within themselves, said to them, "Why do you question thus in your hearts? Which is easier, to say to the paralytic, 'Your sins are forgiven,' or to say, 'Rise, take up your pallet and walk'? But that you may know that the Son of man has authority on earth to forgive sins"—he said to the paralytic—"I say to you, rise, take up your pallet and go home." And he rose, and immediately took up the pallet and went out before them all; so that they were all amazed and glorified God, saying, "We never saw anything like this!"

Mark 2:1–12 (See Matt. 9:1–8; Luke 5:17–26)

Jesus, we are told, had returned to Capernaum, where he was making his home. News of the power of his ministry had now become widespread. People from outlying regions heard the stories of Nathan and others like him—of men and women who were delivered from their bondage and healed of emotional and physical illnesses. Many had come this day to the seaside village, some bringing ill friends or relatives with them. Quite a number of people had gathered at the house where Jesus was staying. Not all of them could get inside, and so a large group stood outside by the front door hoping for a turn to see and hear Jesus.

One has the impression that the crowd outside the door might have been somewhat unruly. Those who had come a long way would have been disappointed and frustrated that they could not talk directly with the teacher. Some fervently desired to hear just a few words from Jesus, believing this might change their lives. From time to time they called out

9

or pleaded with those inside to make room for them. Likely others were there who were mostly curious—anticipating that something extraordinary might happen, and just wanting to be wherever a crowd gathered. A few may have been looking to find fault with this man of whom others spoke so highly and who seemed to be critical of the recognized religious leaders.

It appears that these crowds sometimes worried Jesus.[1] The message about the coming kingdom was so easily misunderstood and misrepresented. People readily fastened onto what they saw as the miraculous aspects of his ministry, as though he were meant to be a kind of magician. More and more frequently he was being asked to perform a miracle, to conjure up an act of healing as a demonstration to prove who he was.

The temptation to respond to such human craving was strong. This is the point of the Gospel story in which what may be seen as the greatest temptation offered by the devil to Jesus is that he jump from the pinnacle of the Temple and land unharmed in the courtyard below (Luke 4:1–13).[2] So might he compel faith by the force of the miraculous. This power, Satan recognized, would be even more coercive of human allegiance than either the control of food or the control of wealth and military might. Who would dare doubt or not bend the knee to displays of supernatural force? One could master bodies *and* souls with such godlike feats. "Man," Dostoevsky's Grand Inquisitor cynically maintained, "seeks not so much God as the miraculous."[3]

Yet miracles undertaken on Satan's terms would be a form of magic based on the desire to have transcendent power in human control rather than to put human life in the service of God and of others. Jesus vigorously refused to display his healing art only as a means to compel belief in either himself or the powers of the kingdom. To the direct request that he offer these *signs,* Jesus is said to respond, "An evil and adulterous generation seeks for a sign" (Matt. 12:39; 16:4; see also Luke 11:29; Mark 8:12. "Adulterous" is used here in the Old Testament sense of false relationship or false worship.[4] The demand for such signs is a way of seeking after other gods, or another kind of god than the Lord of Israel.) "No sign shall be given to this generation" (Mark 8:12).

It seems just as clear, however, that Jesus saw the triumphs over evil forces that took place through his ministry as indications of the character of God's approaching reign. "But if it is by the Spirit of God that I cast out demons, then the kingdom of God has come upon you" (Matt. 12:28; Luke 11:20), he responds to those who accuse him of acting by the power of Beelzebul. While the healing exorcisms are not proofs for the otherwise incredulous which are to be performed on demand as a function of human religion, they do manifest themselves as gifts of promise to those who are hoping that God's ruling power can penetrate the human situation. They are symbolic acts which at first were not intended to create faith but to point to the kind of faith that the advent of the kingdom called forth.[5] To those who have eyes that can truly see and ears that can truly hear these deeds offer deep insights into the character of God's sovereignty. In this sense Jesus' activities do become signs which reveal the nature of God's rule, and the Fourth Gospel thus describes them. The other evangelists frequently, however, prefer to speak of the healings as "acts of power" (Greek, *dunameis*, from which our word dynamite is derived). They are little explosions or break-throughs which reveal the kingdom's purpose.

It may well have been about the meaning of the healings that Jesus was teaching on the day that Jonathan was carried into town by his four friends. For the moment, their thoughts would have been little attuned to such matters. Although they were pleased by the feat they had accomplished, what they were mostly feeling as they arrived in Capernaum under the noon-high sun was tired and hot. It had been a more difficult journey than they had imagined down to the lakeside from their little village in the hills. The litter they had rigged with poles and leather straps had not seemed uncomfortable in the beginning, but in many ways it was more difficult to carry such a stretcher downhill than up. The weight distribution was often uneven, and they had to walk very slowly on the steeper stretches to avoid slipping. They could not keep a rhythm in their steps, and the last mile or so had clearly been painful for Jonathan as well as for themselves. Mind you, though, the last thing they were looking forward to right now was the uphill journey home. Unless . . . if Jesus could heal him.

Jonathan and his friends must have cared deeply for one another, although on most occasions they hid their affection under their horse-play and banter. They had grown up together among the same hills and valleys, tending sheep when they were themselves hardly bigger than the lambs after which they ran. As they grew they had all become strong and robust chasing across the sloping pastures and later working in the fields. They competed with one another and rejoiced in the vigor of their bodies.

This was why it was so difficult for them to understand what had happened to Jonathan—why he had fallen sick and so suddenly become unable to walk. They kept thinking he would get over it. They tried to help him exercise his legs, but even the slightest movement hurt a great deal. He appeared to be wasting away before their eyes.

His personality had seemed to alter too. Probably that was largely due to the confinement and worry about his future, but it had been difficult for his friends to watch when they knew what he had been like before. His dark, handsomely sculptured features grew morose as he blamed himself for what was wrong with him, and he remained silent for longer and longer periods. Oh, there were still sparks of his old self, some joking if the friends stopped to throw the dice with Jonathan on their way in from the fields. But then someone would make a remark about one of the local girls, and there would be an awkward break in the conversation. Too often what laughter there was became forced. It was not the same between them, and the friends realized that they had begun to find reasons for not stopping by.

Three of them were there, however, one evening after Sabbath. It was then that they hatched their plan to take Jonathan to see the new prophet Jesus when he next came to stay in Capernaum. In a way they expected it to be only a lark, an excuse to get Jonathan away from his house and to demonstrate their strength and endurance by carrying him all the way to Lake Galilee and back. Yet it was to be more than a lark, too. Both David and Zechariah had heard Jesus teaching, and they had talked to several persons who had claimed to be healed by him. True, they had also seen people who had come away from meeting Jesus still obviously crippled or diseased. But maybe they felt a little better. There could not be any harm in trying and Jonathan was at least willing. His es seemed to regain some of their old sparkle as they talked of making the trip.

But now, as they trudged the last few yards down the dusty path toward the house, it was Jonathan who was trying to keep their spirits up. He cracked jokes about how much he depended on them and how he did not want to be a burden. The others, however, only grunted in response. David especially was in real pain. He was slighter than the others to begin with, and several miles back a sandal had broken and he had badly stubbed his toe. It was still oozing blood, and it looked like he would lose the nail. But he was not the only one who was hurting. The whole business had started just after sunrise, and they had thought surely they would arrive before the morning was over.

They found some shade and with a "one, two, three" lifted the poles from their shoulders and set Jonathan's pallet as gently as they could on the ground. They looked glumly at the crowd assembled about the house and stood for a few moments trying to think and to work the kinks out of their shoulders and neck muscles. After coming all this distance, they had to find some way to bring Jonathan to Jesus. But it was apparently not going to be easy.

Jonah went to find some water, and the rest of them sat gnawing on the bread and cheese they had brought. As soon as Zechariah had caught his breath, he went over and talked to a small group standing with the others about the door. He returned disheartened. Many had been waiting several hours, he reported, and they did not seem in a pleasant mood or willing to let Jonathan be taken in before them.

The four friends brooded and tried to come up with some ideas. Perhaps it would be sensible to figure out a way to stay over until tomorrow, though they had brought neither enough provisions nor enough money.

It was the irrepressible Abner who first suggested the idea of climbing up on the roof and making a hole large enough to lower Jonathan down. At first they kidded him about it, but they kept picking at the idea, challenging one another until they slowly passed over the line and realized they were seriously making plans.

It took persistence and the audacity of youth to borrow the equipment they needed. With handsome smiles and promises of return they were able to secure several strong sharpened sticks and two suitable lengths of rope, while Zechariah managed to look into the house to get an idea of where Jesus was standing.

Like most of the houses in town, this one had an outside stairway that provided easy access to the flat roof.[6] The four friends hoisted the litter back onto their shoulders and began maneuvering around the edge of the crowd toward the stairs. Jonathan, who had at first acceded to the scheme, now began to voice his doubts. They did not know how they would make a hole large enough to let him safely through. As much as he wanted to hope in Jesus, he was worried that the disruption would only anger the teacher. And, though he did not say this aloud, what if Jesus did pray for him to be healed and nothing happened? Or, what if he were able to move only a little, and the pain was excruciating?

Abner laughed and told him all he had to do was lie back and prepare to drop in for a visit. David reached down with his free hand and squeezed Jonathan's shoulder. "Don't give up," he whispered. "We haven't come all this way for nothing. He can heal you!"

Jonathan had to squint against the sun. The bed tilted as they started up the steps. He managed a fragment of a smile and licked the perspiration from his upper lip. He tried to hang on to the pallet and to his hope.

Those pressed together in the heated atmosphere of the house realized right away that something was happening over their heads. Their attention to the teacher was broken by scuffling noises, and then voices and what sounded like scratching and wrenching. Jesus stopped speaking and looked up with the rest of them. "Here comes the kingdom now," someone commented, provoking laughter and a few nervous giggles. Suddenly, accompanied by an oath, a foot and then a leg up to the knee came crashing through the ceiling. There was more heaving as old branches and straw were pulled back. Several words of bickering followed, and someone called down to Jesus. A big chunk of clay fell and shattered on the floor. Then the litter was eased through the hole.

Feeling both silly and frightened Jonathan clung to the side poles for dear life. The pallet slanted so steeply that for a moment he was terrified he would slip and fall on his head. He kept his eyes shut to keep out the dust and because he did not want to see. There was a sudden twist to the right which, when overcorrected, nearly pitched him off the other side. His legs jerked and hurt. But he forgot that too as he banged down the last few feet, rattling his teeth and knocking his breath away.

There was stunned silence. It was an extraordinary moment. If ever Jesus was upstaged in his ministry, this must have been the time. Bits of dirt and straw still filtered down. Anxious faces peered through the hole at the mess they had made. The crowd was divided between anger toward these bumpkins and apprehensive curiosity. What would Jesus say to these fools? Jonathan was too overcome to think much of anything. This was not at all as he had imagined it. His heart was beating wildly as he tried to recover his breath. He looked up at the healer helplessly.

Several people began coughing in the dust. Jesus glanced up again at Jonathan's friends. He then held the paralyzed young man in his gaze and said, "My son, your sins are let go."

One of the elders gasped and turned muttering to himself. This was going too far even for a prophet. This was blasphemy! Who did he think he was? It was clear in the scriptures and in the tradition that God alone could forgive sins.

Jesus looked deliberately about the room. "Why do you reflect like this?" he asked. "Is it easier to say to this paralyzed man, 'Your sins are let go,' or to say, 'Stand up, take your bed, and walk'?"

All the whispering had stopped. Everyone was watching. Jonathan himself did not know what to think or to imagine. He had come to the prophet to be healed of his hated paralysis, but Jesus had appeared instead to want to speak about his sins. But now . . . Jesus' words seemed to be questioning, probing, searching, moving deep within him . . . offering him a new possibility for his life.

And then Jesus spoke again. "In order that you may know that the Son of man has authority to forgive sins on earth"—he turned back to Jonathan—"I say to you, stand up, take your bed and go home."

Imagine what happened next from the point of view of David and Zechariah, Jonah and Abner as they gazed down through the hole. They saw their friend's awestruck face as he pulled his legs up and, rolling on his side, slowly began to put his weight on them. He stood. He reached down and folded up the stretcher. He walked! He walked out of the house!

Once again we cannot pretend to explain just how such a cure could have taken place. The power for healing which Jesus brought to focus may well reach beyond any of our efforts to comprehend, although we shall later, through this and other stories, attempt to understand this power better, since disciples are intended in some measure to share in it.

Yet we are meant first to hear the story, not to explain it. In this retelling we have tried to see and feel the event from the point of view of the paralytic's friends, whose faith and perseverance were so crucial to the healing, and to some extent also to hear the story from the point of view of Jesus' opponents and of the crowd. For a few minutes the reader or hearer is invited to share in their hope, their weariness, frustration, puzzlement, anger, uncertainty, and finally in their joy and amazement. But foremost, of course, we are meant to play the role of the paralyzed man—to be Jonathan.

I try to imagine myself stretched out on the floor with all those people, mostly strangers, staring at me. I feel like a tiny child; all others are much bigger and stronger. I am helpless and dependent, my legs useless. I am somewhat fearful, although there is also a kind of inner lassitude—a not wholly unpleasant awareness that there is not much I can do, that I must entrust myself.

It reminds me of several lengthy periods I have spent in hospitals. There I am in bed in something like pajamas. People speak to me in hushed and rather condescending tones. I must believe they want to help me, but I am not sure they really care about me. They also say they need to hurt me, although I should know this is for my own good. Pain and the fear of pain further concentrate my sensitivities and isolate me.

When one is sick or injured a good measure of personal dignity and sense of identity are forfeited. Jonathan would not have been able to eliminate without help. One has little control over what or when one eats. To eat and sleep in the hospital one must fit into the institutional regimen. One can no longer do many of the activities by means of which personality is established and maintained. Only through the eyes of others can one learn of what is happening even just down the hall. The unaffected limbs and aspects of mind grow weak from disuse. Most sense of personal attractiveness or dynamism is lost. Many times in the hospital one's clothes are taken away. The dress is standard issue— open at the back, sexless and defenseless. Perhaps one is waiting for an operation. Soon there will even be a loss of consciousness—possibly of life itself. One can only wait and hope against fear.

For Jonathan the dropping through the hole in the roof is psychologically and spiritually a form of letting go—even dying. He is passing from one world to another, losing contact with his friends as he is lowered. The manner in which they dig a hole, let him down, and peer anxiously after him reinforces the imagery. They are losing their power to help him.

The passing through the hole and the dropping downward can also represent a falling into the subconscious, such as often happens in bouts of fever and after anaesthesia. One dreams. One comes into contact with forgotten memories. One may even for a time regress to earlier life stages. But the memories, the images and symbols, do not interrelate as in conscious life. There is no surface direction or logic. The language of the subconscious does not submit any obvious meaning. Again one has lost a greater or lesser measure of control.

Here, however, one may also begin to realize positive dimensions to the experience. To be in touch with the subconscious can also bring a person into a more complete relationship with the total self. The poet that is in each of us may return from this journey bearing rich treasures for reflection and creativity. The letting go allows us to participate in the circus of our deep emotional life. The interaction between our ordering, conscious life and the uncritical three-ringedness of the subconscious fashions profounder understandings of the fullness of the self and all human life.[7]

But by no means is everything pleasant in the journey to the subconscious. The circus has its wild animals, its crackling dangers and tragic clowns. Bad memories shout in the voices of the crowd. When the cages are opened we sniff terrors. Yet to shun the circus is to avoid the wholeness of life and to live unaware of forces that may otherwise control much of what we do. Ironically the one who does not from time to time lose control and fall into the subconscious world may end with the least awareness of life. Such experiences are one way in which we lose our lives and find them. It is here we may meet the demons that can haunt and paralyze. But it is also here that these demons may be recognized, confronted, and challenged.

We may imagine that we have glimpsed something of the psychological, spiritual, and physical condition Jonathan was in as he lay there, bits of dust and straw still drifting down on him. He felt vulnerable—his whole being exposed, and he was dependent on the man standing above him now who totally filled his vision. Jonathan recognized that the man was the healer, but he also realized that he would feel pain in the healing process. He hoped and he feared. If he could have run away, he might have; but he could not.

Jesus looked on Jonathan and apparently perceived a wound deep within him—a type of wound that he may have discerned in every human being. In his inner self Jonathan was traumatized by an awareness of guilt and a sense of unworthiness and unacceptability. While not all illness can be explained in these terms, it becomes increasingly evident that though such wounds may not cause a sickness, they may often decrease resistance to illness and inhibit healing in many persons.[8]

Jonathan may at first have been surprised by Jesus' words, even somewhat disappointed. He had come to have his body healed, not to be forgiven of his sins. But the deepest wound, Jesus insisted, and the wound that might otherwise cause irreparable damage, had to be dealt with first. Jesus treats this ulceration of sin with the utmost seriousness. He does not offer Jonathan a bandage or a mild palliative—does not suggest to him that he can simply forget. Jonathan has really sinned. In his self-centeredness he has caused anguish to others. Not all the consequences of his acts can be undone. His sins have cut him off from a true relationship with others, with his own life forces, and with the source of all life. "Christianity," Thomas Merton wrote, "is a religion for [those] who are aware that there is a deep wound, a fissure of sin that strikes down to the very heart of a man's being. They have tasted the sickness that is present in the inmost heart of man estranged from his God by guilt, suspicion and covert hatred."[9]

That sickness is serious, but it can be healed. It must be confronted and challenged directly. It would be of no lasting help to Jonathan to pass over his sin—to heal him physically and then tell him everything is fine when it is not, to pretend that his sinfulness does not injure himself and others when it does.[10] He is a sinner. But Jesus declares to him that his sins are *let go*. (The Greek word, *aphienai,* means to forgive, but it also has the root meanings of letting go and sending away.)

Jesus' detractors strenuously object. No human being can do this for another. Only God can forgive sins.

Jesus pronounces and enacts his powerful and challenging response. Forgiveness is indeed a divine activity. The full letting go and sending away of sins cannot be accomplished by human beings acting only on their own authority. Self-forgiveness—no matter how hard we pretend it—is beyond our grasp. Neither psychological therapy nor the words of friends are strong enough to cleanse all guilt resulting from the pain we have caused others. But, Jesus claims, God's mercy is not far distant, or limited to the heavenly realms or a future last judgment. It is even now present in the world, acting through human agency, to heal and bring new life.

Specifically it is in the world—"on earth"—through Jesus as the Son of man.[11] The origin of this designation "Son of man" is uncertain, but it had come to refer to a humanlike figure who would appear in heavenly glory to manifest God's judgment.[12] It is the contention of our story that Jesus is that Son of man, here and now in his human person authorized to set forth God's will, and that will—to the surprise and even consternation of many—is to offer forgiveness and acceptance to all manner of people in all kinds of circumstances. Forgiveness is God's free and recreative gift to all who turn to him. In the story of the paralytic and throughout the Gospels, Jesus is seen offering God's new acceptance to prostitutes, tax collectors, the ill and the maimed, beggars—the very people who were often considered (and who perhaps considered themselves) outside of God's care and forgiveness.

No wonder there was consternation. For many religiously minded folk there had to be rules and limits. Some sins, some habits and ways of life, had to be unforgivable. Not everyone could be considered among God's chosen people—at the very least not until they had clearly repented and begun to live according to God's law. But Jesus spoke and acted otherwise. Invited to the joy of the kingdom's banquet were the "poor and maimed and blind and lame" (Luke 14:21)—those whose conditions and illnesses were often considered signs of sin. The kingdom's offer of forgiveness included "both bad and good" (Matt. 22:10). Jesus' special concern was for those who most needed the message of the kingdom. "Those who are well have no need of a physician, but those who are sick; I came not to call the righteous, but sinners" (Mark 2:17). If the old religious message was, in effect, *Be good, and you may be forgiven and found acceptable,* the new message is, *God forgives you and accepts you into relationship with him; now be good. Now you can be good.*

And even more, Jesus evidently bade his disciples to do likewise. At the conclusion of his version of the story of the paralytic's healing, Matthew makes this understanding explicit: "The people were filled with awe at the sight, and praised God for giving such authority to men" (Matt. 9:8).[13] Not only the Son of man but all men, all who knew the good news of God's inbreaking kingdom, were authorized to tell of God's surprising grace and love. In later years Christians would retell this story and use it for warranty to say to Jews and Gentiles, to slaves and free men, to the sick and the sinful along with the pure and the law-abiding, that their sins were let go. And the controversy would continue.

But would all who had physical illnesses also be healed of them? New Testament scholars who have analyzed the narrative of the paralytic's healing suggest that two originally separate stories were brought together from the tradition to form the one story now found in Mark 2:1–12. It is not difficult to see how one might skip directly from "When Jesus saw their faith" in verse 5 to "he said to the paralytic, 'I say to you rise, take up your pallet and go home'" in verse 10. Read this way we might trace the outline of two separate incidents: one involving a healing, the other a controversy regarding the forgiveness of sins. On the basis of this analysis and of other stories in the Gospels one could maintain that sometimes Jesus healed without specific reference to the letting go of sin, and that sometimes he forgave sins without physical healing. There is no doubt, however, that he did engage in both activities, for both are firmly rooted in the tradition.[14]

It was also clearly the experience of the early Christian communities that not every offer of forgiveness resulted in physical healing. Sometimes physical healing happened; but always, it was believed, the experience of the forgiveness of sins led to a renewed way of life. This is one of the reasons why the whole, integrated narrative in Mark 2:1–12 conveys such important psychological and spiritual truth, whether or not it was originally one story. While not every illness may or should be considered the result of sin and guilt, we know that the letting go of sins can release a new faith and an energy for life that affects both emotional and physical being. This is a fact of life that many people have experienced. The story enacts this truth, and the *resurrection* of the paralytic's physical wholeness is the sign, in his life, that his sins have indeed been forgiven. Salvation and healing, whether of the spirit or body or both, are integrally related.

This truth is succinctly expressed in other New Testament stories where the Greek word *sōzein* is used to describe a healing. The word has several basic meanings: to be preserved or rescued from danger or death, to be freed from disease, to thrive or prosper, and to attain salvation. Genuine healing is not just a cure *from* some malady; it also brings about new purpose and meaning *for* life. The story of the paralytic tells us of the power of God's kingdom acting through Jesus to bring both healing and salvation.

The priority of emphasis in the story must not, however, be lost sight of. Jesus asks, "Which is easier to say to the paralytic, 'Your sins are forgiven,' or to say, 'Rise, take up your pallet and walk'?" At first the question itself seems easy. Surely it is less difficult to say that sins are forgiven than to tell the paralyzed man to get up and walk. Yet, after a bit of further reflection, the choice becomes less clear. There were, after all, others in Jesus' time who promised physical cures and even miracles, just as today we are promised physical cures by doctors, therapists, psychic healers, or dieticians. Gifted healers of the body are of great value, but those who can renew hearts and spirits are far more precious. The greater and more profound *miracle* is the one that opens the way to salvation. The physical healing, important as it is, is but the outward sign of the power of the kingdom's grace.

By the inclusion of the controversy about forgiveness of sins within this healing narrative, by the use of repetition and grammatical stops and starts, the story ingeniously builds suspense and presses home its explicit and implicit questions upon us:[15] How can sins be forgiven? Who can forgive sins? Are Jesus' words blasphemy? Can this person be healed? Which is easier to say? What is the relationship between sin and sickness? forgiveness and healing? Who is the Son of man? In those moments, as the questions hang in air, we may play the various parts in the story. We may be the troubled religious leaders whose deadening paralysis of soul is made evident as they sit there questioning in themselves. We may be the friends whose faith and daring action, in contrast to the scribes, have made this moment possible.[16] Or we may just be part of the watching, listening crowd. By being the healer we may realize how the controversy at the heart of the story is meant to foreshadow Jesus' own suffering and death which will be followed by his resurrection.[17] Above all, we can recognize our own form of paralysis—that which in us is tending toward death—and then experience a new life arising.

Jonathan's story ends here. The bed, the symbol of his illness (to which he was affixed and which also was a burden to others), is now in his power. He rises up to new life, collapses the pallet, and carries it lightly on his shoulder. Next he will need to find himself a pair of sandals!

And Jesus sends him home—restored to his family and community. But he is not just as he was before, nor are his indomitable friends. We do not know what opportunities he encountered in his later life or what further trials and pain he endured, but in our last scene we may picture Jonathan heading back up into the hill country with David, Zechariah, Jonah, and Abner—the five of them, walking and laughing together while holding in awed and grateful hearts their new treasure.

3 | ZACCHAEUS

He entered Jericho and was passing through. And there was a man named Zacchaeus; he was a chief tax collector, and rich. And he sought to see who Jesus was, but could not, on account of the crowd, because he was small of stature. So he ran on ahead and climbed up into a sycamore tree to see him, for he was to pass that way. And when Jesus came to the place, he looked up and said to him, "Zacchaeus, make haste and come down; for I must stay at your house today." So he made haste and came down, and received him joyfully. And when they saw it they all murmured, "He has gone in to be the guest of a man who is a sinner." And Zacchaeus stood and said to the Lord, "Behold, Lord, the half of my goods I give to the poor; and if I have defrauded any one of anything, I restore it fourfold." And Jesus said to him, "Today salvation has come to this house, since he also is a son of Abraham. For the Son of man came to seek and to save the lost."

Luke 19:1–10

Zacchaeus, we are told, was a chief tax collector. He lived in the town of Jericho and was rich. It is not surprising that he was wealthy. A chief tax collector would have had responsibility for a fair-sized district, and Jericho was the center of a fertile agricultural area. There were also groves of palm, balsam, and sycamore trees, the wood of which was a valuable commodity. It was a pleasant area in which to live, the winter climate far milder than that of Jerusalem. Kings and other dignitaries had second homes in Jericho. Because the area was a strategic gateway for the eastern trade of Judea, there had been a city in the general vicinity for thousands of years. It was often well garrisoned with soldiers.

Much money was to be made by a tax collector in such circumstances, since his authority gave him license for a special form of entrepreneurship. Most of the tax collectors of the time (whom we might better think of as toll collectors) entitled themselves to the right to collect levies on the transportation of property in a given locale by first paying an advance fee for this privilege. They then sought to make a profit on the transaction. The more money they could exact the greater was their

23

profit. There was, of course, considerable opportunity for bribery and extortion. A toll collector made it his business to know other people's secrets. A clever toll collector was a kind of private detective—a spy into other people's affairs. He would have had a special fund to buy informers. And Zacchaeus was a chief tax collector.[1] He even spied on the other collectors.

His job would not have made him a beloved figure with the local populace. But to make matters worse he was, for all intents and purposes, an employee of a foreign and occupying government. His ultimate taxing power came from the Romans. Although they had to respect his wealth and power, his own people saw him as a turncoat and treated him as a traitor. Not only the general populace but the religious officials looked at Zacchaeus as unclean or "dirty."[2] He was a force to be reckoned with, but a sinner. It was a joke among them that his name meant "the righteous" or "pure one."

Zacchaeus' relationship with the Roman officials was different, but no better. To the officers, under whose pleasure he served, he was a convenience. It was much better to have one of the shrewd locals, who had intimate knowledge of the people of Jericho and their affairs, collect the tolls and keep check on all the assistants than to have to do this themselves. They knew he was cheating and getting too healthy a cut on the side. But they also received their share of the spoils, and this was a small price to pay considering the over-all revenue involved. They were glad to use him, but they never forgot that he was one of the Hebrews with their strange customs and ideas—and not even a loyal one at that. His sycophantic way both amused and disgusted them. Better a proud Jew than this bootlicker. They had to deal with him, but as far as they were concerned that was the extent of it.

Zacchaeus was a lonely man. To add a little further insult to his life, he was not very tall. Although one would think he would have accepted his short stature by now, it still aggrieved him considerably. He just did not cut an imposing figure despite expensive clothing. On days when he tried out his finery, he suspected that people laughed at him.

In retrospect, he was probably surprised from beginning to end by his behavior on the day that the recently famous—some would say notorious—prophet from up in Galilee came through town. He had heard about this Jesus several days before. The prophet apparently claimed that the ruling of God was already begun on earth, and it was said that he could heal people and change lives just by his preaching. There were not many exciting happenings in Jericho. Zacchaeus was only interested, he thought, in seeing what the man looked like.

Zacchaeus had not exactly planned his life this way. His father had been a tax collector before him. He had sort of inherited the job and been so good at it he had found promotion. Sometimes he wondered, if he had had it to do over again—if his father had been someone else—whether things would have turned out differently. When he was younger, he had been very ambitious. Yet, as he grew older, he had begun to realize that there ought to be more to life than just a bigger slice out of the tolls each month. If he let himself think about it, he really hated being so cut off from everyone. The things he could buy were nice, but it would also be nice to have some real friends. Maybe this Jesus would have a word or two that was worth hearing. In any case it was a curiosity.

He could hear the stir, and people shouting at the gate of the town. Others, however, were already lining the street in front of him, and he could not see over them. In a flurry of excitement he forgot his position and office. Running ahead, dodging and weaving among the bystanders, he looked for a place on the roadside. Unable to find one, he impulsively hiked up his tunic and scrambled into the low branches of a sycamore tree.

It may be helpful for a moment to sense this scene as part of the crowd . . . curious, their noses twitched by a hazy hope, yet with a pinch of cynicism mixed in. It was good to take off work for a few minutes and have a break in the humdrum. There was a bit of excitement here. Every couple of years someone came through town—usually on their way up to Jerusalem—claiming to be a prophet or a revelation of God or something else special. This one was supposed to have a good reputation. It was rumored that he could actually heal, and that he wanted to open the kingdom of God to the *people of the land*—the so-called unwashed who admittedly didn't keep all the religious laws. Some said that this was what made certain of the officials angry. They maintained that he was making light of the law of Moses. But then many of these same officials weren't much help in aiding others to keep the law—the Torah.

One thing that interested everyone was whether he would stay in

Jericho and with whom he would spend the evening. It would be a great honor. Something of the prophet's holiness would sort of rub off on the house he visited. Perhaps it would be with a distinguished elder or the family which went up to Jerusalem for at least one of the major feasts each year.

Zacchaeus glanced across the street and saw old Isaac. He imagined that Jesus would probably want to stay with him, that is, if he would have him. You have to be pretty special to be able to associate with the likes of Isaac. For Zacchaeus, Isaac did not even have a greeting, and now he began to feel more than a little foolish clinging to his slim perch with his scrawny legs dangling. He could imagine how he must look to Isaac and others—still a bit out of breath and red of face. He had been eating too much, too, and he could feel the perspiration damp on his jowls and sticky on his flanks.

Down the way there was a shout and Zacchaeus caught sight of the little band coming up the dusty street with the crowd closing in behind them. Just as he thought: there was nothing at all distinguished about either the group of followers or the one who must be Jesus—the one people kept trying to talk to. As they drew closer Zacchaeus's expectant but practiced eye looked him over. He evidently had a certain authority about him, but he was also ordinary appearing—his clothes nondescript. Still holiness, Zacchaeus realized, could not be found in a person's clothes. And there was something about his face.

There is at this point a feature of our story that cannot readily be explained. Jesus looks up into the sycamore tree, sees Zacchaeus, and is able to call him by name. Perhaps, by this means, the evangelist wished to indicate that Jesus possessed more than ordinary human power. Otherwise we could guess that Jesus and Zacchaeus had actually met before. Or maybe Jesus had inquired of someone in the crowd. It has been suggested that Levi, Jesus' disciple who had himself formerly been a tax collector,[3] would have known Zacchaeus and been able to tell Jesus his name. In any event Jesus seems to have known about the significance of addressing a person by name. "Zacchaeus," he called out, "hurry and come down. I must come and stay with you today."

Zacchaeus could hardly believe his ears. In those lands and times to share someone's hospitality was a sign of great trust. Jesus was accepting him—him, Zacchaeus, the tax collector, despite all he had done and even though he was short and not very lovable. He jumped down from the tree and hurried to receive Jesus joyfully. As he ushered the prophet toward his home he was already making plans for the dinner party he would give later that day.

All around there were whispers—murmurs such as Jesus had heard before. "He has gone to stay at a sinner's house." But Zacchaeus was no longer a sinner!—at least no longer just a sinner. He stood before Jesus a different man. "Listen, Lord," he said to Jesus, "half of my goods I am giving to the poor; and, if I have cheated anyone of anything, I am going to pay back four times the amount." "Salvation," Jesus announces, "has come to this house today! For this man too is a son of Abraham, and the Son of man has come to seek and save what is lost."

Of all the stories in the New Testament the story of Zacchaeus may offer the clearest insight into the character of the healing power of the kingdom Jesus proclaimed. Through an extraordinary act of acceptance and forgiveness Zacchaeus finds himself to be a changed human being. That Jesus' act worked so rapidly may surprise us, but that a gesture of acceptance can alter life will not surprise many of us at all. We have seen it happen, perhaps more slowly, over a period of days or months. But we have seen it happen.

Jesus' readiness to stay with Zacchaeus did not mean that he thought everything about Zacchaeus was right. But it did mean that Zacchaeus was recognized as a full human being who had a great need for belonging (for he too is a son of Abraham) and sharing in his life.

At first we might think that Zacchaeus's pride and defensiveness would offer little room for such acceptance to transform his life. He must have developed a fairly thick skin to have achieved and kept his position over the years, and doubtless he was reasonably well practiced at rationalizing his deeds. But Jesus spotted something. Very likely it was Zacchaeus's climb up into that tree.

It was a childlike thing to do, which could be read as a sign of his willingness to imagine a different life for himself. In his hope that he might find a new perspective, Zacchaeus forgot himself: his dignity, his role, his clothes—the facades of importance he had so diligently structured. For a few minutes he lost his tight grip on his greed and began to feel what he truly needed and wanted.

Such occasions may come unexpectedly and with great suddenness. In our desire to discover whether another person can care for us we may act in ways that seem totally out of character. Too often the other individual may be unready, unable to respond, perhaps even unable to hear or see our need. If meeting is to take place, the other person may also have to act outside of his or her usual role.

The risks are so great that societies are frequently structured so as to minimize the possibilities of childlike expression and the chances of true encounter. Religious practices and customs are also highly ambivalent, on the one hand expressing the human wish to meet and be met by God and one's brothers and sisters, and, on the other—because of the risks involved—offering ways to counterfeit and hide from this very meeting.

There is an amusing story in this regard about a country woman who came to the big city for the weekend. Familiar only with the less formal worship of her town, she decided she wanted to go to a fancy church like the city folk did. She chose the most imposing and fashionable appearing building she could find. Much of the service, however, did little to affect or move her. The talk was stilted and the music did not even make her want to tap her foot. But then, rather to her surprise, the preacher man got going. He really did begin to talk about sin and love. She felt the Spirit stirring within her and forgot where she was. Jumping up on the pew she hollered out, "Hallelujah, I got religion!" Quickly one of the pinstriped ushers came to her side. "Please, madam," he whispered, "this is no place to get religion."

Obviously there are many ways to express deep religious feeling, but Zacchaeus's story reminds us that sometimes we must let go if we are to do more than act out expected roles. That is hard. Most of us do not feel we are dignified enough. We have to worry about how others perceive us and, most important, how we perceive ourselves. We are terrified that we might be laughed at and then see ourselves through the derisive eyes of others. The popular expression "I'd rather be caught dead" exemplifies the fear that controls much human behavior. We will do almost anything in order to keep from being regarded as foolish.

Which, of course, is foolish. In our more perceptive moments we become aware that it is our elaborate posturing that is truly unwise. The demands of apparent dignity prevent us from telling a friend how we feel, from dreaming out loud, offering our trust, or crying out for the forgiveness we crave. In the name of adulthood we forfeit the childlike capacity to let go of self-consciousness and so be able to give word and gesture to our deep feelings. Religion at its best offers us this opportunity, and, in the story of Zacchaeus, we are witnesses to an open-air religious service. Zacchaeus's climbing of the tree is as profound a religious activity as one can find in any cathedral or tabernacle. His posture of imagination and risking hope provides just enough opening for Jesus to meet him.[4]

The childlikeness in the scene continues in Jesus' spontaneous response to Zacchaeus's unspoken longing. It pours out in Zacchaeus's joyful reception of Jesus and burbling offer to give half his goods to the poor, and "if I have cheated *anyone* of *anything,* I am going to pay him back *four* times the amount!" This could prove to be a promise hard to keep, but one does not doubt the sincerity with which it is made. This is what the gospel message means by *metanoia*—a repentance that includes a changing of the mind, a new outlook on the present and the future.

One is reminded of Jesus' insistence elsewhere that one must receive the kingdom of God like a child (Mark 10:15). Since the New Testament also urges us to put away childish attitudes (1 Cor. 13:11), to count the cost of becoming disciples (Luke 14:27–28), and to seek maturity in Christ (Eph. 4:13–14), we recognize that a distinction between childlike behavior and mere childishness is important. Maturity includes and gives full place to one's childlike character.

Zacchaeus accepts the kingdom when, through Jesus' acceptance of him, he receives it as a child does a gift. When a child receives a gift the eyes light up. There is no attempt to calculate whether it has been deserved. The wrapping paper is ripped away and the joy and gratitude are effusive. Now watch an adult receive a gift, especially one that is unexpected. The eyes narrow. *What have I done to earn this?* Or, *what is now expected of me in return?*

Zacchaeus, of course, does promise restitution and a new behavior, but these promises are outpourings of thanksgiving and not an effort to merit what has been given to him. Acceptance and forgiveness are acts of hope and trust. Jesus has offered himself. Nothing is *required* in return.

Yet, forgiven much, Zacchaeus can now forgive. He is released from the anxiety of greed—from the lust for possession, not only of enough but more than enough (which is breeding ground for much of the economic injustice and warfare of the world). He is free to use money in a new and uncalculating way. This is the point of his extravagant offer for the poor and any he has defrauded.[5]

One can, of course, say that this was Jesus' game all along, and also maintain that the parent's intention in giving is to bind the child in gratitude.[6] Such understanding, however, involves counting the score of the game without realizing how it is meant to be played. There is a way of caring which demands nothing of the other person, though once this love is accepted and the relationship is entered into, everything one has may seem too little in response.

In our lives we see such caring and forgiveness offered imperfectly, sometimes as little more than masks for other people's need to try to manipulate and control. Yet it is the point of stories about Jesus' acceptance and forgiveness of people like Zacchaeus that in their Lord's acts the disciples glimpsed a power that could heal and reform lives.

This was the power of the kingdom. Through such healings the new age was heralded. In Jesus' ministry God's ruling power was disclosed. Jesus did more than just talk of God's readiness to forgive and accept, he personally acted, offering his own presence and acceptance as a sign of God's. One of the clearest impressions that emerges from the Gospel records is that Jesus was out among the outcast, extending the possibility of the kingdom to individuals whom many thought unworthy of it.[7] He entered their houses and ate with them.[8] "Why does he eat with tax collectors and sinners?" his opponents ask (Mark 2:16; Luke 5:30; Matt. 9:11). This was a major *scandal* of his ministry that could also surprise and upset his disciples, and it is among the reasons that Jesus has continued to be seen as the champion of the disadvantaged and the liberator of the oppressed.[9] But the invitation to a new kind of life broke through all categories and stereotypes. Not only the destitute and poor, but also prostitutes and tax collectors were included in his care. Jesus seemed remarkably unconstrained by what others inferred about him from the company he kept. While Zacchaeus had taken his risks by climbing into the sycamore tree, Jesus took even greater risks by so freely, even recklessly, embracing people like Zacchaeus. These acts (along with such stories as the one related by Luke just a little earlier [18:9–14] contrasting the humble tax collector with the Pharisee so confident of his righteousness)[10] seem to have been among the factors that cost Jesus popular support, at least among certain groups, and in the end cost him his life. But just as Zacchaeus was *seeking* "to see who Jesus was," Jesus "the Son of man [had come] to *seek* and to save the *lost*." Like the shepherd who leaves the ninety-nine sheep to go and find the one that is *lost* (literally, "on the way to destruction"),[11] Jesus goes to extraordinary lengths to open the kingdom to the outcast. This parable (Luke 15:3–7; Matt. 18:12–14) too is told by Jesus in response to those who complained of him that "this man receives sinners and eats with them."

However difficult they found it to emulate Jesus, the disciples did remember and retell stories like this one about Zacchaeus. These were the enacted parables of Jesus' ministry. He not only told parables, he acted them out. He expressed God's activity in his person as well as his words. And so, for his followers, he came to be seen not only as the bearer of God's Word but its articulation in human life. He was the Word of God, God's chief parable. The thrust of this understanding led Christians to claim that God had chosen to be most distinctively present in the world in a human person.

Probably there are some who find that God's power described in such human terms does not seem sufficiently supernatural to suit their religious sensibilities. They may be accustomed to imagining healing forces that are more mystifying and esoteric, less personal—perhaps analogous to electric or magnetic energy. Yet the story of Zacchaeus can be seen as a form of parable for the whole of the gospel: God's primary means for the healing of individuals who are diseased by sin and guilt is the power of caring and forgiveness. It is expressed in human life, but its ultimate source is the creativity that sustains all life. In this sense it is both natural and supernatural. In Jesus the disciples perceive a distinctive focus of that power, helping them to glimpse through his humanity the divine character of love, the personification of the kingdom's activity.

But "the God movement" (as Clarence Jordan translates "the kingdom of God")[12] does not stop there. Jesus commissions his disciples to carry on the proclamation of the kingdom and the healing ministry.[13] Having experienced forgiveness and acceptance as Zacchaeus did— beginning to know the power that is released when one is freed from the bondage to guilt and anxiety of greed—each disciple is to extend through his or her person the offer of the same possibility to others.

Because we are only beginners we often fail. Sometimes we do more harm than good. It is very easy—in the name of Christian ethics—to fall back instead on the reformer's stock in trade and try to change peoples' attitudes by playing on their guilt and fear. (*Your determination to defend your privileges against the needs of the poor is sinful. Unless you help them, someday the vast hordes of the underprivileged will rise up and take away your wealth.*) Such methods are alluring and deceptive because they do work for a little while. People's behavior can be changed to a degree by these means for as long as one can keep the pressure on them. Yet by these methods they are being moved backward and not forward. Sooner or later—by subterfuge if not openly—they will dig their trenches, refusing to move further and perhaps firing back in retaliation.

We are aware, too, of our failure to heal in situations where it seemed the power was available to us—where a word or a gesture would have meant the beginning of reconciliation. Yet we were as dumb as Nathan and as paralyzed as Jonathan. We go forth in the morning determined that we will not let the insecurities of our own egos come in the way of opportunities to help others. We shall assist the group to which we belong by making the first offer to compromise and sacrifice. But we return home in the evening shaking our heads. What offers we made were frequently so encumbered by our own implicit requirements and demands that others quietly disdained them or treated them as gambits in an unending game of make-believe about human relationships.

Such days are reminders that unaided we lack the power to deal with the forces that bind and blind human hearts. The power which is necessary, though incarnated in human lives, cannot be generated by our wills and determination alone. First and then again and again the gift character of one's own healing must be experienced. It is this which enables one to enter other situations of sickness and there to offer healing as an unencumbered gift, without strings attached.

Often the possibility of this ministry comes alive for us in a story. We experience life's color and passion when we meet or hear of others who have been healed. Seen in this light a story like that of Zacchaeus is not just an illustration of what might be more directly expressed in other ways. Rather it is through such narrative that the gospel happens. The story is the gospel.

The story may present experiences of life that in their detail are very different from our own. It may take place in another land and time, to a person of a different sex and age. We may be invited by the story to step outside our own customs and acculturation in order to see and feel from a quite different perspective. The story we most appreciate forces us to play a role in the narrative—to try on another's clothes and to perceive new relationships and possibilities for life. The story will then intrigue us and hold our attention to the extent that we discover parallels and congruencies with our own experiences. It absorbs us as it allows us also to participate as ourselves, to remember and perhaps reshape some incident from our past, or to imagine our future.

One might choose from any number of plays, movies, novels or biographies to confirm these reflections. Before us we have the story of Zacchaeus, a tax collector who lived two thousand years ago in a vastly different society. Yet we were able in some sense to *become* Zacchaeus in the story, to see life through his eyes and so come to appreciate him as being someone like ourselves (which is on the way to coming to love our neighbor as ourselves). We understood and sympathized with him, and began to overcome the prejudices we may have had against him.

Then for a few moments his story may very well have become part of our story. We tasted the dust from the street, sniffed the excitement in the crowd, and perhaps remembered shinnying a lamppost. We hiked up some tunic of ours and climbed to see what we could see. To do this we, of course, also had to become childlike. In some measure we had to let go of the critical faculties which insist on the reality of the here and now in order that we could *play* in the story.

We may also have thought of unsatisfactory aspects of our lives: how we wished things could be different for us and that we might ourselves be changed in our attitudes and behavior. And possibly we heard ourselves being offered acceptance and in our joy began to believe that we could feel a new power for life and make a new beginning. This, of course, is a major purpose of such a story. Those who told and many who retell such stories are not content to talk about healing. In the hearing of the story it is believed that healing can happen. There is healing in the story.

Zacchaeus's story is thus one of the model or master stories of the Bible. Together with other biblical materials it is set forward not only as a source of revelation but as a catalyst for further revelation in our lives. Through their retelling and rehearing, the biblical stories are meant to be in a dialogue of exchange with our own stories. They are the code experiences intended to help us shape and interpret the texture of our lives—what happens to us as individuals and communities. They are the incentives encouraging us to discover and share with each other our own moments of gracefulness, of forgiveness, of hope in the face of tragedy, and of healing. All of us know such stories. In sharing them we share the good news of the gospel.

Of course, all the stories are in an important sense incomplete because they are parts of lives that only experience wholeness and fulfillment in partial ways. Zacchaeus's story like our own is full of gaps and unexplained characteristics. There are ambiguities, mysteries, and surprises. This is among the reasons we continue to rehearse and retell them in the theater of our minds and with one another. There is always something new to puzzle over and some feature to be perceived afresh.

It has been said that life is what happens to us while we are making our plans for it. That is what so suddenly happened to Zacchaeus when salvation came to his house, and he was able to be recognized as part of the true house of Israel.[14] He had run on ahead to see who Jesus was. Then Jesus called to him, "*Hurry,* come down, for I must stay at your house *today*." So Zacchaeus "*hurried* down." "*Today* salvation has come."

We too come to learn that the unexpected moments of our lives are often opportunities for gracefulness. The chances for the most growth come frequently as gifts in what may seem like the interruptions of life. In many of Jesus' parables and the stories about him, it is through the unexpected that the kingdom happens and the new time begins. Even now! Now is the time one can be like Zacchaeus. Now one can be like Jesus in offering acceptance to another.

4 | LEGION

They came to the other side of the sea, to the country of the Gerasenes. And when Jesus had come out of the boat, there met him out of the tombs a man with an unclean spirit, who lived among the tombs; and no one could bind him any more, even with a chain; for he had often been bound with fetters and chains, but the chains he wrenched apart and the fetters he broke in pieces; and no one had the strength to subdue him. Night and day among the tombs and on the mountains he was always crying out, and bruising himself with stones. And when he saw Jesus from afar, he ran and worshiped him; and crying out with a loud voice, he said, "What have you to do with me, Jesus, Son of the Most High God? I adjure you by God, do not torment me." For he had said to him, "Come out of the man, you unclean spirit!" And Jesus asked him, "What is your name?" He replied, "My name is Legion; for we are many." And he begged him eagerly not to send them out of the country. Now a great herd of swine was feeding there on the hillside; and they begged him, "Send us to the swine, let us enter them." So he gave them leave. And the unclean spirits came out, and entered the swine; and the herd, numbering about two thousand, rushed down the steep bank into the sea and were drowned in the sea.

The herdsmen fled, and told it in the city and in the country. And people came to see what it was that had happened. And they came to Jesus, and saw the demoniac sitting there, clothed and in his right mind, the man who had had the legion; and they were afraid. And those who had seen it told what had happened to the demoniac and the swine. And they began to beg Jesus to depart from their neighborhood. And as he was getting into the boat, the man who had been possessed with demons begged him that he might be with him. But he refused, and said to him, "Go home to your friends, and tell them how much the Lord has done for you, and how he has had mercy on you." And he went away and began to proclaim in the Decapolis how much Jesus had done for him; and all men marveled.

Mark 5:1–20 (See Matt. 8:28–34; Luke 8:26–39)

"I tell ya, it was the scariest thing I ever seen happen, and maybe just about the worst too. It still makes all the hair on the back of my neck go all creepy when I even thinks about it.

"Y'ever been up that way—up from Gerasa 'long about the big lake? Well, if ya haven't, I'm not sayin' ya should bother. We was only up there 'cause we heard they didn't harvest their fields too clean, and that there was some other stuff pigs might eat.

"I s'ppose on a sunny day it might not be too bad. But all the time we was there I never did see old Sol for more than five minutes. Big dark clouds kept comin' up from over the lake, and the wind would blow stiff and real cold. And three or four days runnin' we got rain in the afternoon. Nothin' real heavy, but it came at ya all on a slant, into your eyes.

"Well, it wasn't rainin' then. This was pretty early in the mornin' sometime, but it was still kind o' dark like it could rain. I was up there with my buddies—Timon and Antony and Nicanor. Maybe ya know some of 'em, 'cept old Nick's gone now. May the gods leave 'm in peace.

"Some people say we exaggerated, but I bet we must've had nearly two thousand of those pigs when we put our herds together. They was all rootin' 'round, doin' things pigs do. We had a fire goin'—tryin' to keep warm—and wasn't payin' much attention. Only thing we had to worry about was these kind of steeplike places near the shore. We didn't want any of them pigs gettin' too close and slippin' down.

"Like I say, we was pretty busy with the fire and some beans we was tryin' to cook—doin' some talkin' too. That's probably why we didn't take no notice at first, 'cause otherwise from where we was you could see a long ways out over that water. I think it was Nick who saw 'em first, just comin' into this little bay, not too far from us.

"They was takin' down the sail, but still movin' 'long at a good clip. They had this real strong wind pretty much behind 'em. There was some good swells. Too many of 'em in the boat too, if ya ask me. Not that I'll tell ya I know much 'bout boats. Ya'd never catch me out in one, 'specially when the wind was up. Not unless I had to, and maybe not even then.

"We watched 'em for a minute. They came in toward the shore pretty hard. A couple of 'em had to jump out to sort of brake the landin', but they still hit a fair bump. There was some rocks down there too. But they looked like they was makin' it all right. I waved to 'em, 'cept that Antony says they looked like Jew boys—so they probably wouldn't have nothin' to do with us. Not that I give a fig.

"They started up this high bank down the shore a ways, and we went back to the fire. Next thing I knows there's this guy all shoutin' and screamin'. We could hear 'm clear over where we was. I found out later he'd been hangin' 'round up there for months. Nobody could do nothin' about 'm, not I guess that they much wanted to. I mean, he looked wild and acted real dangerous.

"They tells me they once got a gang of people up there and tried to get 'm chained up. But they couldn't manage. I mean he was strong—crazy strong. They even says he busted a coupl'a chains they got on 'm. Mind ya, I don't know that for a fact, but I can believe it.

"They left 'm pretty much alone after that. Guess he spent most of his time 'round there. I didn't know it then, but they used some of those big rocks over there to bury people under. And that's where mostly he would hang 'bout. I guess that would show he was crazy enough right there, and probably talkin' to the spirits of the dead too. Leastwise they told me that's what he did.

"At night and sometimes even in the day they would hear 'm howlin' and cryin' out somethin' fierce. When somebody'd see 'm, he was cut and bruised like he'd been fallin' down and bumpin' into rocks. Must've either been pretty sick or crazy mad with himself to do that.

"I could see that for myself. He comes runnin' over the hill yellin' like a wild fool and, I mean, he had hardly anythin' on. Filthy, he was, too, and ya could tell he was plenty strong.

"Turns out one of this bunch that just landed was s'pposed to be a holy man and a healer. I don't know nothin' 'bout that stuff. I'll just tell ya what I saw with my own eyes. This crazy guy goes whoopin' and hollerin' and falls on his knees before the holy fella. From a distance it sounded like he was sort of arguin' and pleadin' with 'm at the same time. Mind ya, I can't exactly hear anythin' they're sayin', but afterwards I asked one of those other fellas that came up from the boat with 'm.

"He tells me right away the crazy guy knows their leader is a holy man. Knows his name: *Jesus,* or one of them other Jew names, and says he's the son of the Most High God, if ya can believe that. He's all tremblin' and scared 'cause this Jesus has told the unclean spirit, which he thinks is causin' the craziness, to come out of 'm.

"So he's scrabblin' 'round on his knees, askin' not to be tormented and Jesus tries to get 'm to talk some sense. He asks 'm his name, and the guy—still crazy—says, 'My name's Legion.' I guess from what they said this was 'cause he thought he had a whole bunch of demons in 'm.

Or maybe he was tryin' to trick the holy fella by not givin' his real name; I couldn't tell ya for sure.

"Anyway—and here comes the really terrible part, and the part I bet ya won't believe: this Legion, or whoever, starts pointin' 'cross toward us and our pigs, yellin' and whinin'. Could be the demons in 'm was still tryin' to outsmart Jesus in some way. I guess they have to have somethin' to live in. I don't know 'bout that, but I sure do know how they can get inside things and make 'em act crazy. And that's what must've happened, 'cause all of a sudden them pigs start behavin' real strange. You can say it was 'cause this guy was shoutin' and throwin' 'mself 'round so. All I know is they started churnin' 'round, and then—before we had a chance to get properly worried—the whole bunch of 'em takes off, so fast ya wouldn't believe. They head right for the steepest part of the bank—sort of a cliff there.

"I thought maybe I saw a couple of the ones in front try to slow up. But they don't see too well, and, in any case, it was too late. The ones in back pushed 'em and the others followed, the whole bunch of 'em squealin' and rollin' down into the water. Even though the beasts can swim a little, 'twarn't a one of 'em managed to get up out of there. No shore to climb up on.

"Maybe a few of 'em did get away. Ran off in another direction or somethin'. If so, we never found 'em. We was so mad and scared at the same time. Nick wanted to go over and talk to this holy guy and find out what the devil he was up to. But it was too strange for the rest of us, and we didn't want nothin' to do—just us few—with that bunch. For all we knew, maybe he could do somethin' really strange to us too.

"Nope, we got ourselves out of there mighty fast—fast as our feet could carry us. Went back to the village and told 'em 'bout it. First off, they thought we was crazy too, though they could see somethin' pretty scary had happened to us. I mean, we was jumpy. I still can see that guy pointin', and then them pigs runnin' like mad.

"Finally, we agreed to go back with 'em if enough of 'em would come 'long. When we got there, would ya believe, everthin's all peaceful—like nothin' had happened. Here's this crazy guy sittin' there talkin' to Jesus and the others just like it was any afternoon. He's got somebody's cloak on 'm, and all the madness is gone out of his eyes—all calm and collected. But, of course, there warn't none of our pigs anywhere. I could'a laughed and cried all at the same time.

"I don't know if the folks from the town believed us then or not, but they knew 'bout this guy who'd been crazy, and they realized somethin' pretty weird had happened. They wanted this Jesus and his friends to get the hell out of there. So did we, 'cept we was still plenty mad 'bout the pigs. I mean, I never been able to get another job herdin' the muckers.

"It might've gotten ugly but, like I say, we was scared of 'm too. We didn't know what he might be able to do to us. So we ended up just kind of beggin' the whole bunch of 'em to go away. They didn't seem to care much and started back for their boat. Of course, the guy who was crazy wanted to go with 'em, but it seems Jesus wouldn't let 'm. Told 'm instead to go home to his friends and tell 'em how good their god had been to 'm. I heard a year or so ago that he's still 'bout, not too far from here—still tellin' people 'bout Jesus.

"That's the end of my story too. Ya'll find some people who'll say we just made it up to explain how we lost all them pigs. It don't make no difference to me anymore. I can tell by the look on yer face ya don't know whether to believe me either. I don't much care if ya do or don't."

Told from any point of view this is a bizarre story. It is a measure of the gulf between our age and the time of the early Christian communities that the narrative is rarely heard or discussed in churches today. It does, however, have a prominent position in the first three Gospels and has all the marks of a tale that people loved to retell and hear again. It is probable that through repeated narration various elements were added and others abbreviated or dropped for the purposes of preservation in oral tradition.[1] Quite possibly, up until the time that the tradition began to harden into a fixed form, it was expected of narrators that they would embellish the story with their own invention and colorful details.

One notices many of the characteristics of the folk tale. Two thousand seems like an exaggerated number for the pigs. Hearers of the time would have much enjoyed features such as the unclean spirit(s), which had so tormented the man, now begging for mercy. What a delightful turn of the tables! And they would have found much pleasure in the imperious manner in which the demons were banished into the herd of swine. Perhaps they thought they would be finding safety for themselves. What a fine outwitting of those little devils![2] And what a fitting punishment for such tormentors of people. The total reversal of behavior in the formerly crazed man and the baffled, terrified anger of the herdsmen and townspeople would also have occasioned satisfaction and amusement. Despite the seriousness of the underlying themes, it is in many ways a comic tale, especially as right becomes triumphant and order is restored.

Those who study popular narratives of healings and exorcisms have noticed characteristics or stages in the development of a story which are often present in their fully developed *form*.[3] First, the problem or illness is described. The story tends to grow in the direction of making this as serious as possible in order to emphasize the magnitude of the miracle and the grandeur of the miracle worker. (There would not be much point in having someone come to a healer with a runny nose or a headache.) There is, for instance, a tendency in retellings to make ill people dead, which is about as sick as they can get.

Second, the plot presents some measure of conflict or tension which provides colorful contrast and helps to dramatize the denouement. Often this is accomplished by describing the mockery or disbelief of the crowd in the healer's power. There may be an emphasis on the resistance of the one who is to be healed or on the resistance of the evil force within.

Next, the method of healing is described. In some of the religions and philosophies that thrived around New Testament times this was done in great and loving detail. Pseudoscientific methods were sometimes employed with incantations added.

In the fourth step evidence is offered that an exorcism or a healing actually has taken place. The patient gets up, or sneezes, perhaps eats something. Or the demon on the way out knocks over a vase or otherwise indicates its fleeing presence.[4]

Finally, "the others"—those who originally disbelieved—are convinced, overwhelmed by the cure and the power of the healer. There is awe and amazement.[5]

I can remember learning with some chagrin about the tendency to add this last feature to a narrative, though in a different context of oral tradition. When I was in the fifth grade our teacher gave us an assignment to tell the rest of the class about some historical event. When the day for performance arrived, I was suddenly and painfully aware that I had forgotten to prepare, and my name came too near the beginning of the alphabet to hope that I might be spared until another day.

Being a quick if not industrious student, I hit upon the idea of making use of the Gettysburg Address, which my father had once encouraged me to memorize. When my turn came, after offering a few scanty remarks by way of introduction, I proceeded to declaim Lincoln's speech. When finished I was glad to note the beam of approval in Mrs. Halstead's eye. "And how, Fred," she asked, "did the crowd respond to President Lincoln's address?" I had no idea. But calling again on my quick wit, I responded, "Oh, they all clapped and everything for a long time." Which of course is precisely what they did not do.

My mistake, however, illustrates the inherent tendency to shape our narrations in the direction of our general expectations. There is a movement toward pattern, which the Gospels' versions of the story of the Gerasene demoniac also indicate—especially in the description of the madman's behavior, his possession by an entire legion of demons,[6] the *proof* of the exorcism, and the awe, fear, and later marveling of others. A stated element of disbelief in Jesus' power is not evident, but tension is provided by the demoniac's effort to ward Jesus off ("What have you to do with me?")[7] and to trick him, and by the stress on the impossibility of any human agency's being able to do anything to control or help the man. A greater power is needed. Will even Jesus be able to overcome these forces of evil?

The aspect least present in this story is a description of the method of healing. While the Gospels do on occasion record a word or two that was reported to have been said[8] or tell of Jesus making a kind of healing plaster from spittle and clay,[9] their brevity or reticence in this regard is often noted.[10] There is little interest in the scientific or magical aspect of the means. By contrast, one can point to popular modern as well as ancient stories of exorcisms or healings which often concentrate attention on words, gestures, amulets, or potions, sometimes mixing in astrology.[11]

There seem to be two reasons for this reticence in the Gospels. First, there appears to be a continuing control from an authentic reminiscence of Jesus' own attitude. The healings and exorcisms were indications that the kingdom of God was begun, but they were signs to those who were already hopeful, not to the incredulous. Jesus appears to have actively shunned sensationalism.[12] This downplaying seems to have been continued by the synoptic evangelists in their studious avoidance of words then in common use that would have stressed the spectacular aspects of such stories. We have seen that the word they preferred (*dunameis*) might best be translated "acts of power" rather than miracles. The emphasis fell not on how such things happened, but on the belief that these events were little eruptions of the power of God into the world. Each healing was a kind of enacted parable pointing beyond itself to the activity of God.

Although the later tradition of storytelling in the churches was more tolerant of features appreciated in folk narrative, the general atmosphere of the unsensational is preserved. From the evangelists' point of view, the stress rightly fell more and more on Jesus, in whose words and deeds the kingdom is perceived as coming. This tends to keep the focus off the acts themselves and especially the means by which they were done. One is to be attentive to the one who heals.

The lack of therapeutic detail is thus an effective way of emphasizing the sovereignty of Jesus' power. He does not need to return to the boat to get an amulet or to prescribe various oaths or pills. His is the strength of God in the battle against evil which needs no special formulas or the aid of magic potions to do its work. The power resides in him and his words.[13] He commands and evil is overcome—even myriad demons, illustrative of the great influence of Satan in this world. They have met their master.

Despite the lack of elaboration about the exorcism, however, the story of Legion is still the narrative that most tends toward sensationalism in our Gospels and shows signs of having been retold for the sheer enjoyment of it. Largely for these reasons it is absent from many contemporary lectionaries for Sunday readings in church, as though to avoid disturbing congregations with such a strange legend.[14] Obviously it presents problems to twentieth-century sensitivities and is not usually considered to be edifying or spiritually uplifting. The exaggeration, the high-handedness, a worldview which includes demons, and the wild implausibility of their teletransportation all inhibit our hearing.[15] Likely most offensive is the matter of the pigs. The cruelty and the waste of all that ham and bacon appalls us. Among other things, it is unecological!

Probably, we are also growing aware, however, that by this attitude we are rather missing the point, at least if we are to share in any way with the earlier hearers of the stories. They were not asking questions about whether it all happened or how it happened. Their predominant interest was in what the story told about Jesus and the effects of the power that focused in his ministry. The details had their real purpose in sharpening the interest and deepening the significance of the narrative.

Our solicitude for the pigs likely provides the best example of misplaced concern. To fasten on them rather than what has happened to the man is to distort the early narrator's purpose. They are a way of objectifying what was primarily a psychological and spiritual event. They are first and foremost part of a story. From a Jewish (and Judeo-Christian) perspective they were used precisely because they were considered unclean animals in which no Jew would find any value. It would be the same as a contemporary narrator's sending the demons into a swarm of annoying mosquitoes. Perhaps we too might laugh as we were told how they rushed to their destruction.

What is needed for the genuine rehearing of earlier myths and legends and for the sharing in something of their power and purpose is a willingness to listen to narrative as story.[16] Our scientific and historical concerns have their place and can give us a multileveled appreciation of all a particular narrative can mean. Yet we could miss many of the levels of significance in the story if we attempted to reduce all its features by the denominators of literal questions about historical accuracy and medical and clinical psychological understandings.

We have already pointed to several of the themes that would have been of primary interest to the early audiences of such a story. They would note the self-destructive power of evil: how it causes one to wound oneself. They would appreciate the banishing of the evil forces into the sea, figuratively returning them to the chaos from which they came.[17] In that abyss they can do no further harm to human life. But the concentration is on the victorious power of Jesus who is able to vanquish the powerful and multifarious legions of evil in the world. To those living amid much unexplained suffering and ambiguity it would be a joy to hear this story as a sign of God's ultimate lordship over evil. It is important to recognize that in Mark, Matthew, and Luke this tale is part of a sequence of *acts of power* by Jesus—helping the reader to understand who he is. In Mark and Luke our story is followed by narratives in which a woman is healed of a long-term illness and a young girl is brought back from (or from beyond) the brink of death (Mark 5:21–43; Luke 8:40–56). In all three of these Gospels the immediately preceding story tells how Jesus, when out on the lake with his disciples during a storm, ordered the wind and the waves, "Peace! Be still!"— bringing about a great calm. The disciples are then asked why they were afraid and lacking in faith before the storm. The story concludes with his followers in awe and wondering, "Who then is this, that even wind and sea obey him?" (Mark 4:35–41; Matt. 8:23–27; Luke 8:22–25).

These motifs, especially the focus on Christology (who Jesus is and what is the character of the power he brings with him), are intended to carry over into the story of Legion. The same one who commands and controls the sometimes threatening forces of nature also has authority over the forces that can form a maddening tempest in a man's mind. Jesus heals them both.

The implications are that Jesus is closely related to God and that his power to bring peace and order to the outer and inner worlds of human experience is to be understood as divine in origin. Those in the evangelists' audiences who knew the Jewish scriptures would not have missed the obvious comparison with the God who at creation mastered the sea of chaos and ordered the world.

> You have set the earth upon its foundations,
>   so that it shall never move at any time,
> You covered it with the Deep as with a mantel;
>   the waters stood higher than the mountains.
> At your rebuke they fled;
>   at the voice of your thunder they hastened away.
> They went up into the hills and down to the valleys beneath,
>   to the places you had appointed for them.
> You set the limits they should not pass;
>   they shall not again cover the earth.
>
> (Ps. 104:5–9)

This is the same God who, in response to seafarers who called to him in distress,

> . . . stilled the storm to a whisper
> and quieted the waves of the sea.
> (Ps. 107:29)

The parallels in the Gospels are direct allusions leading toward the understanding which the fourth evangelist presents still more explicitly when he identifies Jesus as the Word of God—the creative, expressive power of God which was with him "in the beginning" (John 1:1–5). It is the essential life force that formed and sustains the universe which is being revealed in the ministry of Jesus. The manifestations of this power in this age are signs that the new age has begun. In Jesus, God's restoring, renewing strength is beginning to be made known.

Yet there is struggle between the one who wields God's power and the forces of disorder and madness. Indeed, in the presence of divine goodness evil forces are whipped into frenzied effort. That this battle involves powers that are beyond human comprehension is indicated by the capacity of the personified forces of evil to recognize Jesus as "the Son of the Most High God." While human understanding may not readily perceive the true dimensions of the battle that is waged, this story offers a dramatic disclosure of the behind-the-scenes struggle. Many in the early audiences would have found themselves comforted by this narrative which tells of their Lord's courage to take up this battle and his power to be victorious over the powerful demonic forces. Even if their strength still continues, the story points to the final victory.

Other aspects of the narrative provided further insights. The deep irony of a figure whom others cannot bind but who is self-bound by forces within him would have been appreciated. The evangelists' audiences would have noticed how in the end the one who had been possessed is sent home, enabled to return to family and friends. His madness had isolated and alienated him—left him among the dead as one who was dead.[18] Now he is restored to a place in community. This is particularly marked by his ability to speak intelligibly again having formerly been able only to shriek and cry out.

His restored capability for intelligible speech is also given a ministry as Jesus specifically instructs the man to go and to tell his own people what the Lord has done for him. This is a rather unusual feature in the Gospels' healing stories and underlines a particular function and value of this narrative for the early Christian communities. When the evangelists discovered that they had a mission to offer the gospel to gentile people in gentile lands, they found the paucity of stories about Jesus' dealing with Gentiles an embarrassment.[19] But here was a narrative rich in vital themes. Their Lord did go to a gentile area[20] (where, it is noted by the reference to "the Most High God,"[21] a form of monotheism was at least recognized). Unafraid, Jesus there showed his superiority over pagan demons and the irrationality and disorder they spread; symbolically he cleansed the gentile world by ridding this area, understood to be representative of all gentile lands, of demons in preparation for the spread of the gospel.[22] The man restored to rightness of mind then becomes a prototype for the converted Gentile—not only healed, but now himself able to tell others about what the Lord (v. 19) whom he proclaims as Jesus (v. 20) has done for him. He who was formerly enslaved to his own form of madness is now free to choose the obedience of discipleship.

Many of these features of the story are no doubt also of significance to us as part of the modern audience of the story. We may, however, still find ourselves at considerable distance from the narrative because of its basis in an acceptance of belief in demons and exorcism. While there continue today to be reversions to these ideas among some religious groups and in the popular media, they are for many contemporary persons no longer part of their world view—their understanding of the way things are. Although one may find in the renewed interest in supernatural powers of evil some form of near-desperate effort to rediscover belief in the transcendent (if one can believe in the devil, maybe one can eventually come also to believe in a divine power for good),[23] an attempt to compel belief in demons as a matter of faith would for many today mean turning faith into fantasy.

On reflection, we may recognize, however, that we too have experiences that bear some similarities to those spoken of in stories from the Gospels like that of the Gerasene demoniac. From time to time we also know what it is to feel our lives bound by forces beyond our direction. Like Legion we may be able to break the chains and fetters of many outward constraints, but we do not know freedom. By lust and avarice and demand for success over others we feel ourselves in enslavement to powers that often overmaster our rationality and better desires.

We explain these experiences differently. Through the insights of psychology we realize that within others and within ourselves there have taken place, especially during the early stages of growth, warpings and distensions which can cause certain short-circuitings and aberrations in our personalities. Irrational fears and angers suddenly inhibit our better intentions for our own lives and those of others. Our capacities to forgive, to accept, and to help may seem abnormally limited when compared with our apparent potential. We experience estrangement from what we believe to be our better selves and our true energy for living. We sense a disintegration. There is an alienation from deep relations to others, and a consequent frustration and further anger directed at self and others. And there is resultant guilt and often, even if in disguised forms, self-hatred. We are unable to love our neighbors as ourselves because of our inability adequately to know ourselves as lovable and so able to love. At times the accumulation of all of these forces can seem an overwhelming swarm, a legion of demonic powers.

Sometimes this guilt and anger can lead to covert, unconscious attempts to punish the self. It is becoming increasingly clear that many forms of physical and mental illness are to some degree self-inflicted. Our lack of stamina and inability to recover from disease can sometimes be explained by the draining away of our energies in these internal struggles. In extreme forms, our urge for self-injury may become as obvious as that of Legion. The demonic urge toward self-destruction of person and relationships (to choose death over life as Legion does by dwelling among the tombs) can be terrifying. We have all seen it happen to friends or relatives.

And we recognize such inner forces to be part of ourselves, yet also alien to what we want for ourselves and how we wish to be. Probing reflection and analysis may help us to see that the voices through which these forces can control us sometimes speak in the distorted tones of shapes from our past. Buried deep in the psyche, internalized parental and other authority figures may have grown deformed and seem to us as ogres. If we cannot understand how these might be exorcised, we at least long for a power that can begin to control them, perhaps to heal them and redirect their energies. Many of the folk and fairy tales that conclude with the submission, conversion, or transformation of a monster (sometimes with a kiss or other act of love) are likely born from this hope.

Such reflection based in myth and story can, we learn from modern psychology, have its therapeutic values. There is danger too—the danger that we will lose the awareness that we are in these terms projecting out onto the world what is within ourselves and, in the resultant dissociation, fight only mock battles. What is worse and unfortunately more frequent, the projections may become displaced and cause us to see the wrongful forces only in others—perhaps especially in those of a race or religion different from ours. This has happened all too many times before in history. This misdirection is not, however, the intent of good psychological approaches or of the proper uses of mythology. Both, in fact, use mythological language—modes of talking about the unseen and what cannot in reality be objectified—in order to offer better insight into experience. That is why we need good and constructive mythology and psychology rather than the pretense that we can get along without them. Neither, it must be remembered, is intended to be in any sense irrational. They are meant to offer us ways of relating experience to ourselves and to one another which unaided rational explanation cannot manage.

There is another arena in which we may find some of the mythological language to have significance. Jesus believed the kingdom of God was engaged in a form of warfare with the powers of evil personified in Satan and his minions.[24] There was not only individual illness; disease and disorder were also abroad in society and even in the natural world. These sicknesses, too, the power of the kingdom was meant to heal. It is quite possible that the story of the stilling of the storm was originally intended as an exorcism of a disordering evil force.

Again, we at least know parallel experiences. Our society and world are also disrupted by forces that seem beyond our control and which threaten us and make us fearful. Racism, sexism, militarism, and acute economic injustice so appall us with their power that we often not only cannot resist them but we find ourselves complying with their ways of doing things. We too bow our knee in vain effort to appease these forces. Perhaps we would regard their strength as the accumulation of our neuroses and psychoses, but even then the collective power may well seem greater than the sum of its parts. How otherwise explain the results of Nazism, the Vietnam war, and what has happened in Cambodia?

Peter Hodgson points out how in the Hebraic tradition bondage begins with an interior act of self-deception followed by an objectification of the act "demonically intensifying it, in the oppressive powers and dehumanizing conventions of culture, society and politics."[25] However we try to explain the terrors of our world, we know that something is powerfully awry at the root and heart of life, especially when we see the results of what we thought were our best motives and methods, our brightest intellects and technology, our most devout liberalism.[26] Our search for peace leads us to become the world's chief weapons supplier. Welfare programs become a swamp of hopelessness for the very people they were meant to help. Affirmative action snarls in litigation. Surely the efforts are not wrong in themselves, but at the same time they seem to ensnare us in bondage to the legal, political, and economic means we believed would help to attain these goals.

In bouts of romantic national nostalgia or retreats to hedonistic individualism we try to forget or deny our problems, which only drives guilt deeper and strengthens its unseen, demonic power. We edge closer to the cliffs of despair.

Until recently we might have found that talk about demonic disorder in the larger societal world was merely quaint and based on a primitive and thoroughly outdated mythology. We might have said this until we began to realize the consequences of our unwillingness in any genuine sense to share the needed goods of the world and of our exploitation of the environment. Now we are not sure if there can be a proper use. The resources of the world and its power to cleanse and heal itself appear badly deranged. We grow fearful of our own natural habitat and our future. Perhaps we are slowly turning our planet into a wasteland, while simultaneously we are terrified that in one mad hour we will blow it apart. We lose faith and long for some power to help us reorder, to recreate.

It was to analogous human circumstances that many of the Gospel stories were originally intended to speak. They tell of the power of Jesus in the coming kingdom to free both individuals and societies from the demons—the fear and guilt, the insistence on warfare with one another, the selfishness, the anger and alienation—which otherwise dominate and cripple. At heart the stories attempt to be realistic. There is a great and terrible madness loose in the world. What makes the newspaper headlines are but the surface and symptoms of the real battle. Unaided human strength cannot seem to cope with the tendencies within society to enslave and then destroy itself. To exorcise their demons humans must find both liberation and a source of power greater than their own that can transform their lives.[27] They need to be freed from the strength of evil but they need also to be given a reason for caring and loving.

When people are questioned searchingly about their lives and asked what leads them to the edge of hopelessness and despair, the predominant answers have surprisingly little to do with lack of wealth, success, or health. Instead they speak in various ways about an absence of purpose and sense of belonging. They have no ministries. To cure them of their present physical and mental problems (whether by means of religion, medicine, or psychiatry) will be of no lasting help unless they, in addition, find that purpose and ministry for which they wish to live. This also may be the point of Jesus' story about the man whose unclean spirit had finally left him. The man then allows the demon's former resting place to remain empty, and later the spirit returns with seven other demons. The man's last state is worse than when he began. (Matt. 12:43–45; Luke 11:25–26.)

The hope that people might find both a liberation from bondage and a new freedom for living is set out in the questions and responses used at baptism by those who today would become disciples of Jesus. The striking parallels with the story of Legion are no accident.

Do you renounce Satan and all the spiritual forces of wickedness that rebel against God?

I renounce them.

Do you renounce the evil powers of this world which corrupt and destroy the creatures of God?

I renounce them.

Do you renounce all sinful desires that draw you from the love of God?

I renounce them.

Do you turn to Jesus Christ and accept him as your Savior?

I do.

Do you put your whole trust in his grace and love?

I do.

Do you promise to follow and obey him as your Lord?

I do.

Will you proclaim by word and example the Good News of God in Christ?

I will, with God's help.

Will you seek and serve Christ in all persons, loving your neighbor as yourself?

I will, with God's help.

Will you strive for justice and peace among all people, and respect the dignity of every human being?

I will, with God's help.[28]

5 | THE SYROPHOENICIAN WOMAN

And from there [Jesus] arose and went away to the region of Tyre and Sidon. And he entered a house, and would not have any one know it; yet he could not be hid. But immediately a woman, whose little daughter was possessed by an unclean spirit, heard of him, and came and fell down at his feet. Now the woman was a Greek, a Syrophoenician by birth. And she begged him to cast the demon out of her daughter. And he said to her, "Let the children first be fed, for it is not right to take the children's bread and throw it to the dogs." But she answered him, "Yes, Lord; yet even the dogs under the table eat the children's crumbs." And he said to her, "For this saying you may go your way; the demon has left your daughter." And she went home and found the child lying in bed, and the demon gone.

Mark 7:24–30 (See Matt. 15:21–28)

Andrew was tired. His feet hurt, and his stomach would not stop grumbling. Nor was it very likely that there would be enough food to silence it. Third night in a row!

At least they had a house to stay in and there was a fire. Thank the Lord for small favors, for it surely looked as though more rain were coming. He glanced at his sandals lying in front of the fire. A little steam still wisped from them. In a minute he'd go turn them, and then in the morning, when they had dried, scrape the mud off. It would be harder to get the caked dirt off his feet unless he could find some kind of a basin to warm water in.

He sighed. It would be nice to get home, back to good old Capernaum. These little forays that Jesus wanted to take whenever the fishing was poor had been great fun at first, thrilling even, with chances to try his hand at telling people about the kingdom. Yet on journeys like this the excitement could wear pretty thin. They were out in predominantly gentile territory and a lot of the people they had met recently spoke in accents very difficult to understand.[1] Strange people, too. Andrew did not like the odd ways they dressed and acted. It was not that he hadn't seen lots of these foreign goyim before. There were enough of them

51

around Capernaum and Bethsaida, but they didn't behave quite so differently. And he had at least talked with the ones near home and knew that some of them believed in the one God of heaven and earth. Several even came regularly to synagogue.

It wasn't hard, however, to imagine people they had seen today going home and worshiping idols. If they didn't have them in their homes, then they probably had them in the temples in their towns. Andrew had heard about them, although (Bless the Lord!) he had never seen one. Think of it! Offering sacrifices to grotesque idols made of metal and wood. It was as foolish as it was disgusting. The prophet was right to mock them:

> He plants a cedar and the rain nourishes it. Then it becomes fuel for a man. . . . Half of it he burns in the fire; over the half he eats flesh, he roasts meat and is satisfied; also he warms himself and says, "Aha, I am warm, I have seen the fire!" And the rest of it he makes into a god, his idol; and falls down to it and worships it; he prays to it and says, "Deliver me, for you are my god!" (Isa. 44:14–17)

Andrew smiled to himself. He had always like that passage from the prophet. Such foolishness! Not to speak of the foods they did roast over their fires. Imagine actually eating pigs. He had seen several herds of them today and yesterday. Ugh! No matter how hungry he was, the thought made him sick. Thank the Lord he was born a son of Israel and not one of them. It was no wonder that the message of the new kingdom must be meant only for God's chosen people—those who already knew his name, kept the feasts, and practiced the signs of his gracious favor.

Yet all that was only spiritual sustenance. He was hungry and increasingly uncomfortable on the hard bench. The dirt floor was cold under his feet. He would like to get closer to the fire, to stand for a few minutes with his back to it and to finish drying his cloak.

He looked down to John sitting hunched at the other end of the bench. Trouble was, if he did stand up, the bench could tilt and spill John off. Might serve him right, he thought half maliciously. John always had enough energy and enthusiasm during the day. It was when it came time to do a few chores that he was suddenly all worn out.

John and his brother! "Sons of thunder," Jesus called them. They could be noisy enough, Andrew agreed. It wasn't that he didn't like them . . . love them, when it came down to it. The heavens knew they had known each other long enough: fishing together since they were boys, and all came to be with Jesus about the same time. It was just that they seemed . . . well, a little pushy lately, as though to say that they were closer to Jesus and had a better understanding of his message than the rest of them.

He looked back at John and felt the edges of his resentment soften. It was hard to be angry with him now. He was, after all, little more than a boy. If he wasn't asleep, he was next door to it—his elbows on his knees, his head in his hands. He might be snoring just a little.

It made Andrew wonder what kept them all at it. He supposed for each of them there were different reasons. For himself he knew it was partly the camaraderie, the sense of brotherhood. On good days it was fun to do all these things together. There was excitement too and the importance of the message—the privilege of being associated with it. And then the ecstasy of actually seeing someone healed, a demon exorcised. Yet, when wet and tired and hungry, when the actual results of their work seemed meager, one had to question a little: Was it worth it? Was the kingdom really coming?

It was probably only Jesus who kept them together and kept them going. Although he could become tired as the rest of them—and it was to him, after all, that all the people came with their questions and their aches and pains and requests for healing—still his enthusiasm for the "good news" didn't seem to slacken. Or at least he didn't let it show very often.

Andrew half turned to look at him. He was sitting at a table in the middle of the room, his shoulders a little slumped. He was toying with the oil lamp, his face reflective in its glow. Andrew wished he knew what he was thinking. He often wished this. He wanted Jesus to tell them more. When he first heard Jesus talk and tell his stories, he felt sure he meant that the kingdom of God would soon come in its fullness of power, in all its tremendous glory for the people of Israel. Then the evil would be sorted from the good—the chaff from the wheat, and God's justice would shine forth in splendor. Yet it had not happened. Jesus went on talking the same way, but one had to ask. Andrew wondered if Jesus also wondered. Maybe that was why he did not tell them more.

John groaned in his sleep and Andrew shifted on the hard wood to try to find a more comfortable position. His stomach actually hurt. He hoped Simon and those who went with him would return soon from their foraging expedition—and return having been successful. They certainly needed more food than there was in the house. Nor could they eat up everything this old couple had.

Simon would find something. He always managed to scrape together enough to get them by on, though Andrew was never quite sure how. He hoped Simon wasn't doing any stealing. Actually that was probably one of the reasons why Andrew had come on the trip. Even though Simon was his older brother and a lot stronger physically, everyone agreed that he, Andrew, was the more reliable. Although his mother wasn't pleased with their going, she was at least glad he went too so that Simon would have someone to look out after him.

Andrew felt rather than heard the door open. The draft was cold, carrying with it a sense of the gathering dusk. It seemed a little soon for Simon and the others to have returned. It was then he heard her high-pitched and heavily accented voice: "Which of you is Jesus of Nazareth?"

For a long moment, no one spoke. Then Jesus replied, "I am."

Slowly, Andrew raised himself from the bench. For the moment anyway John did not go sprawling. He slept on. But Andrew noticed that Thomas and Bartholomew were also watching. He turned and saw the woman now kneeling next to Jesus. Although the lamp had been blown out by the draft, he could tell by the firelight that she was a Gentile. She had several bracelets up and down her arms and other ornaments hanging around her neck. Andrew found it revolting that a woman would do that to herself. He didn't doubt that she painted her face too. The goy women were shameless. That's what one got from worshiping idols. Next they practically made an idol out of their own bodies.

She was actually touching Jesus, holding onto his tunic, looking up into his face and talking to him. She was unclean—unclean as a woman and as a goy, and literally dirty. She had bare, muddy feet, and Andrew could see soiled spots on her striped, almost garish, dress.

He moved closer. Jesus wouldn't want him to be rough and he did not wish to be. But this was too much. All day long they had had to put up with inconveniences and interruptions. Now, when Jesus finally had a few minutes to himself, this woman had the effrontery to come bursting in on them. There was nothing that could be done for her anyway.

Andrew spoke up firmly, as much to the woman as to Jesus, "Do you want me to show her out?" Jesus didn't answer. As he looked down on the woman, Jesus' expression seemed more bemused than anything else. Andrew didn't wonder. Although they had become somewhat used to the idea that Jesus would regularly talk with women in public—even about matters of torah, he had never before been thrust into such a compromising position with a goy woman. At the very least it was embarrassing. Couldn't even she see that?

The woman's tone of voice was growing more desperate. Andrew had trouble understanding her because of the accent, but it was evident that her daughter was ill and that she believed the child to be demon-possessed. "Please, Lord, help me," she begged.

Andrew became even more sorry for Jesus. The Master's face seemed troubled. Yet there was nothing Jesus could do. And again Andrew felt the urge to hoist the Gentile to her feet and send her on her way. Sick daughter or not, she had defiled them all.

But Jesus' features now softened, and he seemed almost to smile slyly at the woman. "It is not right," he said, "to take what belongs to the children and throw it to the dogs."

Andrew laughed aloud. That, he thought, was the way to tell her. It was perhaps a little surprising coming from Jesus, but now she knew where she stood with them. The Gentiles were like the little dogs in the house of the children of Israel. Let them have their own religions, at least until Israel first was saved.

The woman, however, only looked more sharply at Jesus. Her eyes grew cunning and her mouth took on a wry smile. "Yes, Lord; yet even the dogs under the table eat the children's crumbs."

Now Jesus laughed, and Andrew heard the others guffaw. The woman certainly had to be given credit for her brassiness. She'd apparently even be a dog if that's what it took to make her claim on the God of Israel.

Andrew stooped and raised the woman to her feet. Jesus now looked at her thoughtfully. For long moments the gaze between them did not break. Finally Jesus spoke to her: "For this saying you may go home happy; the demon has left your daughter."

The woman started stammering out thanks, but Andrew felt they had all had enough. Jesus had at least made her feel better. Taking her arm he led her firmly to the door. He waited for a moment, half expecting she might turn back. Instead she broke his grasp and began running up the road, her stumpy figure outlined against the vestiges of the evening sky. He could hear her bracelets jangling.

Andrew shut the door firmly. Someone had relit the lamp, and Jesus was again staring into its flame.

Now to gain a different perspective, let us read the story as it is told by Matthew in his Gospel and then imagine it from the woman's point of view.

> And Jesus went away from there and withdrew to the district of Tyre and Sidon. And behold, a Canaanite woman from that region came out and cried, "Have mercy on me, O Lord, Son of David; my daughter is severely possessed by a demon." But he did not answer her a word. And his disciples came and begged him, saying "Send her away, for she is crying after us." He answered, "I was sent only to the lost sheep of the house of Israel." But she came and knelt before him, saying, "Lord, help me." And he answered, "It is not fair to take the children's bread and throw it to the dogs." She said, "Yes, Lord, yet even the dogs eat the crumbs that fall from their master's table." Then Jesus answered her, "O woman, great is your faith! Be it done for you as you desire." And her daughter was healed instantly.

I don't even know what to call him, Justa[2] realized, a wave of panic swelling on top of her nervousness. *And so many of these Jews are so superior, especially with women, not to say foreigners. (What is it they say? "Blessed be God that he has not made me a slave, a woman or a heathen.")*[3] *He probably won't want to talk to me, and, if I say the wrong thing, that will finish my chances. But, by all the gods, I have to do something. I promised Bernice I'd try to reach this healer. I can't believe he'd go so far as to come home with me, but there's just a chance he'll give me an oath to use or a potion or little amulet. Darling Bernice!* She was losing her to that frightful demon.

Justa felt the tears darting back, but there was no time for them now. She had to hurry if she was to be at the crossroads where she was told he would pass with his group of followers. She didn't know which one he'd be, what he would look like, or if she could make herself understood. Even the Jews who came from this area had such terrible accents, and he was supposed to be from way over in Galilee.

She wished she had worn something lighter. She was perspiring freely as she forced herself to keep going at a half-trot. But she wanted to look her best for him. She would do anything—anything for her little girl.

What kind of demon could be afflicting her? What caused the shaking and made her so weak, all the life gone from her eyes? It was clearly getting worse. She made no sense when she talked now; she seemed to be raving. The local healers were useless, but she had heard that the Jews could speak directly with their God and that this Jesus was the best of them. *Please be able to heal her.*

She came up over the rise and saw them just passing the crossing. *It must be them. There wouldn't be another group of Jews out here.* She tried to quicken her pace, cursing the long robe and the extra weight she had put on recently. Yet now, she reminded herself, she had to be careful. She must both look and speak piously. Her bracelets jangled and glinted in the sun. She had heard Jewish women were not supposed to wear jewelry. Maybe she should have dressed differently, but she had wanted to impress him. She was no slave woman. Yet now she would arrive like this, almost out of breath, damp with perspiration, and her hair a mess.

Surely they must see her now, but they hadn't stopped. And still she didn't know what to call him. *Some title of honor and respect would be right at the least.* She had heard some say that he might even be Israel's savior—the one they hoped for, the new David. She gulped for air as she came up behind them. "Have mercy on me, O Lord." She gasped for her breath again. "Son of David."[4]

They didn't even turn around. *May the devils take them—Jesus, whichever one he was, and the lot.* Just because she wasn't one of them. Just because she was a woman. He had to help Bernice. She grabbed one of them by the arm. He shook her off as she called out again, "Lord, Son of David; my daughter, she has a terrible demon. Have mercy."

Now they stopped, though still no one spoke to her. Several of them began to confer, talking to the one who must be Jesus. She tried to catch his eye, to smile. *Please, you God of Israel, help a poor woman and her dear daughter. Make this son of yours help me.*

But clearly they were telling him to send her away. She could see it in their gestures and on their lips. They didn't care. *You scum,* she thought angrily. *You priggish, selfish scum.*

Jesus seemed to hold her in his gaze and then took a step toward her. "I was sent," he said, "only to the lost sheep of Israel." He seemed to be trying to explain that he could not help her, but at least he had spoken to her. Thank the gods for that. She had this chance. She threw herself on

her knees, being careful not to touch him. What could she say? Only—
"Lord, help me."

There was a long silence. She could see them all staring at her, wishing she would disappear. Then Jesus spoke again, "It is not fair to take the children's bread and throw it to the dogs." His tone of voice was not unkindly, but his words were like a slap. Yes, she knew, these Jews, like everyone else, thought they had to care for their own first. They were the children; all the rest were the dogs. All right, if that was the way he wanted it, she'd play by his rules. She'd be one of his dogs if he would only help her. "Yes, Lord, yet even the dogs eat the crumbs that fall from their master's table."

One of his followers laughed, but Jesus only looked at her more intently. There was something hard and glinting in his eyes. Was it anger? He opened his mouth, closed it, and then spoke to her quietly but with an extraordinary firmness. "Woman, your faith is very great. Be it done for you as you desire."

Justa felt some enormous release within her, as though great hands had stopped pressing on her chest. For just a moment she closed her eyes and bit her thumb knuckle to make it seem more real to her. She was brimming with hope and joy.

She looked up. They were already on their way again, but he had said it! He had said it! *Bernice would be well. Her little girl was well.* She knew it—knew that the demon had gone from Bernice at that very instant.

The story of the Syrophoenician or Canaanite woman poses difficult questions. The disciples were likely surprised that Jesus would have extended the healing power of the kingdom to a gentile woman. Twentieth-century hearers are likely just as surprised by his hesitant and seemingly grudging response. And it is hard for us even to begin to understand how Jesus could have healed a child who was possibly miles away. That, to say the least, is a mystery.

As we have retold the story, there is no certainty that the woman's daughter was healed, but Mark and Matthew are quite clear about her cure. Yet with their usual economy and lack of interest in our brand of questions, the Gospel traditions give us little clue about how this could have happened. Attempts to account for the healing on some rationalistic or psychological basis falter when we consider the distance between Jesus and the girl who was healed. If one is seeking some background for the story in authentic reminiscence, it could be suggested that Jesus communicated with the daughter through the mother. The mother, given hope and increased faith by Jesus' words, hurried home and shared this healing strength with her daughter. But such an explanation would be no more than speculation, and there is nothing in the evangelists' words to encourage it. This is also true with the suggestion that Jesus might somehow have known that the girl was better and told the mother of this.

Faced with this gap in the story and in our understanding, it may be best to forgo any efforts in the direction of psychological or spiritual interpretation. Unless one wishes simply to maintain that Jesus had at his disposal a capacity radically different from that of other humans (thus raising problems with the biblical faith that "he had to be made like his brothers in every respect" [Heb. 2:17]), it may well be best to leave the matter a mystery and to say that the healing itself is of secondary interest in the woman's story as it is presented by the evangelists.

The story can, however, also raise for contemporary Christians significant questions about the possibilities of trying to reach out to others by caring and praying for them. Often in church, prayers are heard for people in a foreign country. Or we may wish to pray for a friend or relative who is ill in another city. If we can visit these persons, or through prayer better see their true needs from God's perspective and be inspired to send them aid, or at least let them know of our prayers, we may hope that such acts of concern and faith may be of benefit to them. But what could be the value of prayers of intercession for those who do not even know we are praying?

And what should we expect of God's response? We pray, for example, for the safety of Bill and Mary who are on an automobile journey. At first it may be comforting to picture the Spirit of God hovering over all the traffic intersections to be crossed during their trip. Yet, if this is the God who keeps Bill and Mary safe, is he not then also the God who directs or at least allows others to crash?

If we believe in a God who directly controls every single human event, then our theology must see him as specifically accountable for each terrible accident and tragedy along with the good in our world. He determines who will be healed and who not—which of our prayers are answered and which not.

Or we may conceive of God allowing much more scope for human freedom and responsibility, even for chance. But does he then intervene from time to time? On what basis? Does it depend on the fervency of our prayers or the goodness of our hearts?

These are no easy questions. They do not submit to ready answers and they have long been with the human race. The Psalms, Ecclesiastes, the Book of Job, and other biblical writings raise them from a variety of perspectives. We shall return to them in chapter 9—"Paul's Story."

Let us here be content to observe and reflect on one important fact: people continue to pray for one another even when they can do nothing about the situation, perhaps even when they cannot tell the others of their prayers. Some may regard such prayer as outdated theology or even a form of superstition rather than genuine religion. But the fact remains: people want and continue to offer prayers of intercession, and they evidently feel that there is purpose in so doing.

A clue to their possible purpose may be found in Paul's reference to God as the one in whom "we live and move and have our being" (Acts 17:28). God is fundamental and essential to all existence. There is no life apart from participation in divine being. However much God is greater than (transcends) the creation, nevertheless everything that is, shares in his life-giving creativity in such a way that divine being or Spirit is immanent and present as the basis for all life and all life's circumstances. The Bible regards this to be true in a special way for human life which is created "in the image of God" (Gen. 1:26–27).

From this perspective human beings might be said to have an unseen relationship with one another in and through their participation in divine being. Although physically separated, we may still sense a common life, a community. Our prayers for others might touch them through our common participation in the Spirit of God. In the community of prayer, inspired and governed by the divine Spirit, there can be a mutual sharing and caring which reaches out in love.[5]

We could try to develop this understanding into an explanation of how Jesus might have reached through God to the Syrophoenician woman's daughter. His relationship with God was of such a character that he could extend his healing care in an extraordinary way to another. Yet, again, we have no solid warrant for such explanation, and mystery remains. This reflection may, however, give cause for continuing to offer our intercessions for others—those who need support in struggles for peace and justice, in illness and doubt, bereavement and fear—even when we cannot otherwise be present to them. So, too, may we be grateful that others pray for us.

We have seen, however, that the central focus of the narrative is not on the healing as such but on the relationship between Jesus and a gentile or pagan woman and the dialogue between them.[6] This focus may be somewhat obscured for us by all the generations that have passed since it came to be recognized that Gentiles as well as Jews could become disciples of Jesus. Of course, we think, Jesus should have helped the woman! Certainly he should not have refused aid solely because she was not Jewish.

Yet only a little probing beneath the surface of the Gospels and the Acts of the Apostles, along with the help of Paul's letters, reveals the fact that the freedom to offer the kingdom and its healing power to Gentiles was not at all clear at first and was the cause both of controversy and much anguish of heart. There are, in fact, only two specifically identified encounters between Jesus and a Gentile in the Gospels, the other being with the centurion whose servant was ill (Matt. 8:5–13; Luke 7:1–10; see John 4:46–53). Since the churches would have come to value highly such material because it provides a basis and a legitimization for their mission to the Gentiles, one can presume that if there had been more of these stories in circulation they would have come down to us. We can well imagine that the two stories we do have played an important role in the development of this new understanding and opportunity.

Both stories also involve a healing at a distance. This may be the Gospels' way of saying that Jesus did not—at least did not often—deal directly with Gentiles during his earthly ministry. Their healing and salvation was at a distance; that is, it was to come after the resurrection through the ministry of the church. We may also notice that Matthew (in both stories) and Luke stress the importance of faith on the part of the Gentiles. Clearly the stories were used by early Christians to tell how Gentiles could also come to share in the healing and saving power of Jesus.

Mark and Matthew provide the woman's story with a setting that highlights its significance. There immediately precedes a rather lengthy passage in which Jesus denounces the hypocrisy of those who keep ritual law at the expense of the true spirit of the commandments (Mark

7:1–23; Matt. 15:1–20). "You leave the commandment of God, and hold fast the tradition of men" (Mark 7:8). The contention that disciples must go beyond surface appearances and expectations nicely prepares for Jesus' own encounter with the pagan woman. He had given his sermon and now here is a test case for him. What defiles people is not what or how they eat (or, presumably, how they dress or talk or with whom or with what they may come into contact) but what proceeds from the heart. The discussion, with its universalistic tone, would have been regarded as especially helpful to those who were uncertain about the degree to which Jewish customs and regulations were to be required of gentile Christians and the basis on which Jewish and gentile Christians might eat together.

After telling the story of the woman and her daughter, Mark tells of the cure of a man who was deaf and had an impediment in his speech (7:31–37).[7] His healing, done in a gentile region, may be intended to prefigure the power given by Jesus to Gentiles both to hear and to proclaim the gospel. Mark and Matthew next present the miracle of the feeding of the four thousand (Mark 8:1–10; Matt. 15:32–39). Although the numerology in the story is not easy to decipher, many commentators believe that Mark also intends this to be an anticipation of the fact that the feeding of the gospel would extend to the Gentiles. First Jesus answered the gentile woman's plea by healing her daughter, and so he now feeds the gentile multitudes (bread being a Jewish symbol for God's words of salvation).

Although all three of these stories of healing and miracle are depicted by Mark as taking place in predominantly gentile areas, the impression left by the relative scarcity of materials describing Jesus' direct relations with non-Jews remains and seems to be reinforced by the very character of the story of the Syrophoenician woman. It is significant that the Gospel that seems most concerned to cultivate a gentile audience omits this narrative altogether. Perhaps by the time Luke wrote (or at least in his geographical area), the controversy about the admission of Gentiles to Christian community had largely died out. In any case, he apparently saw no need to record Jesus' insulting banter which referred to Gentiles as household dogs.

Matthew, as one of the first commentators on the story, sought to soften the portrait of Jesus by having the disciples first try to send the woman away. Our own first retelling of the story slipped a slice of the same mitigation into the narrative. But Luke, evidently concerned about the sensitivities of both Gentiles and women, *comments* by omission. In doing so he is like many contemporary users of the Gospel records who appreciate the healing aspects of the story but are at best puzzled by Jesus' hesitancy and even sharpness with this gentile woman.

We still ask, could this really have been Jesus' attitude? Did he not intend that the saving power of the kingdom should reach out to Gentiles as well as Jews? Was he so human as to share with many of his countrymen a derogatory attitude toward non-Jews?

These questions do not admit of ready answers on the basis of historical research alone. It has been pointed out that the exchange between Jesus and the woman "is much more a scene of peasant good humor than it is of solemn theological debate."[8] It seems in part in response to her spunk and unwillingness to be turned away that Jesus finally grants her petition. Perhaps, one may suggest, he was initially trying to put her off in the only way he knew how, because of his belief that his ministry was not intended for Gentiles. Still, the barb would have been there.

We do not know his intentions; yet it may not be mistaken to picture Jesus as just this circumscribed by incarnate human circumstances. Israel was God's chosen people. The Jews were the only people prepared to hear and to begin to comprehend the promise of the kingdom's coming. It would be a futile gesture to offer the kingdom and its power to the unprepared.

At least one scholar has suggested that Jesus may have had a kind of program in mind—a plan that many see (although this also is debated) at the heart of the Jewish scriptures. On this understanding it was Jesus' intent first to convert Judaism, or at least part of Judaism, to the kingdom's new possibilities. The reconstituted Judaism would then become a "light to the Gentiles" bringing about their conversion.[9] This might, in fact, be the general program that the evangelist Matthew adopted for Jesus in his Gospel, even though Matthew realized that most of Judaism had not accepted Jesus' message. But this outcome, Matthew indicates, was all part of God's purpose so that the good news would reach to the Gentiles. A similar idea certainly becomes a kind of theme of Paul's ministry,[10] and it is echoed in a different key in the Acts:[11] first to the Jews, and then also the Gentiles.[12] Mark and

Matthew probably seek to convey notes of this motif in their presentations of the story of the woman and her possessed daughter. We
notice particularly "Let the children *first* be fed" (Mark 7:27, italics
mine).

It has, in addition, been suggested that Jesus did not believe the
scheme of events allowed enough time for a gentile mission. The cata-
clysm of the consummation of the kingdom, along with the coming of
the Son of man, would happen too quickly to admit of this possibility.
Especially does Matthew's Gospel contain sayings which support this
view: "Truly, I say to you, you will not have gone through all the towns
of Israel before the Son of man comes" (10:23).

Again, historical research cannot definitively tell us what Jesus
thought about these matters. In this area we must remain at least
somewhat agnostic. Possibly Jesus was himself uncertain. Perhaps he
had no program or clear plan with regard to the Gentiles. His faith and
consummate interest were instead invested in the coming of the kingdom. Since he was a Jew, raised on the Jewish scriptures, he would have
seen this taking place primarily if not exclusively among God's chosen.
Perhaps in his incarnate circumstances his perspective did not reach
much beyond this. His culture reinforced by his religion would have
dictated to him that he refrain from all but the most necessary dealings
with Gentiles. Certainly he should not extend to them, especially in
God's name, any gesture of full acceptance. An analogy in our time
might be the difficulty many find, on the basis of both cultural and
religious teaching, in offering full acceptance to homosexuals.[13] Jesus'
upbringing and environment may have inclined him to look upon
Gentiles as similarly "unclean" and not left him free from the fears and
provincialism which make it difficult for all humans to deal directly
with those who differ from them.

By contemplating these possibilities we enter into what has been
called "the scandal [or the mystery] of particularity." Why would the
universal God participate in history on these terms? Why does he not
find some much more universalistic way to present a better understanding of his purposes? One can respond in part that the only way to
participate in human history is in a particular—and hence a highly
limited—manner. Yet the mystery admits of no ready answers and has
many ramifications.

Christians have differed about the degree to which they believe Jesus was bound and conditioned by his human, historical circumstances, but to see him as genuinely human, one must recognize at least some form of limitation. An understanding of Christianity begins from there—with the incarnate Jesus.

If we interpret the story of the Syrophoenician woman rightly, it could, however, offer us a glimpse of Jesus just beginning to discover one of the implications of the message of the kingdom. He had already begun to include women in his message and ministry in a manner that was extraordinary for the time. But now, seeing the world through the eyes of a male Jew of the first century, he had an even bigger challenge. Perhaps we may not be wrong to guess that this next beginning was also accompanied by some pain and confusion for him.

Jesus deals with the gentile woman as an exception, but that is how breakthroughs start. If his heritage provided him with a kind of rulebook concerning who could and could not be included in the kingdom, we see him, at least temporarily, setting it aside. We can imagine that by allowing his concern to extend out to the woman he began to see from her perspective and to empathize with her situation. Finally he responds, not on the basis of the rules, but to the extraordinary pluck of the woman. Her hope, born of desperation, gives her the boldness to overcome her fear and to break out of her provincialism in order to approach a Jew. And yes, if that is the only basis on which Jesus will deal with her, she will be one of the dogs. It is not out of deserving or merit that she comes, but, if she is one of the dogs, then she at least has that much of a claim to be part of the household too. Her need and love of her daughter and her hope are all she has, but these she will insist on.

Perhaps Jesus recalled his own words to his disciples urging them to be ardent and insistent on prayer ("Ask . . . seek . . . knock" [Matt. 7:7–8]). Perhaps he remembered his humorous story about the woman who so importuned a corrupt judge that even he gave in to her petition (Luke 18:1–5). If such a judge would finally heed human entreaty, would not a gracious God be much more willing? Should not then Jesus, knowing the power of the coming kingdom, feel himself free to respond in God's name to this woman's pleas?

Although this healing act did not by itself make the future course clear, it did seem to indicate that the kingdom might be meant to reach out beyond Judaism. This story was a pointer—not just the words of Jesus themselves, but the Spirit which informed them and the rest of Jesus' life. It was this Spirit which later governed the disciples' reminiscences of Jesus and which, they believed, came alive in them in a new way after the resurrection. It was the Spirit of Jesus—having once lived as a human being, been put to death and risen as Lord—which called his followers forth, in their own limited and difficult circumstances, to begin to bring the healing good news about the kingdom and about Jesus to the Gentiles.

It is fascinating, if oftentimes also frustrating, to watch the movement of this Spirit seeking to transform human lives and events. One sees Peter, for example, haltingly coming to terms with what the power of the Spirit demands of him in his relationship with Gentiles.[14] One watches Paul wrestling with the Spirit and the implications of its disrupting character for his understanding, not only of the role of Gentiles, but the roles of women and slaves as well. Although he can perceive that baptism in Jesus calls forth new relationships through which an exciting unity and equality are born, it is not always easy for him to accept all that this can mean. Nevertheless he sets it forward:

As many of you as were baptized in Christ have been clothed in Christ. There is neither Jew nor Greek, there is neither slave nor free, there is neither male nor female; for you are all one in Christ Jesus. (Gal. 3:27–28)

Again, in our time it is right that this Spirit should be appropriated by many who feel called to try to make new breakthroughs in the barriers built by racism, sexism, and economic injustice. They struggle with ways to liberate contemporary human lives from both extra-legal and legalized forms of oppression and the dehumanizing powers of inequality which breed alienation, extreme poverty, and illness. We should prefer to say that it is the Spirit of Jesus which appropriates them and us, if we will let him. It is the Spirit of the one who healed the Syrophoenician woman's daughter which is still willing to break through, still calling followers to go beyond contemporary mores and legalizing self-limitations to reach out to every person and to heal.

6 | THE MAN WITH THE WITHERED HAND

Again Jesus entered the synagogue and a man was there who had a withered hand. And they watched him, to see whether he would heal him on the sabbath, so that they might accuse him. And he said to the man who had the withered hand, "Come here." And he said to them, "Is it lawful on the sabbath to do good or to do harm, to save life or to kill?" But they were silent. And he looked around at them with anger, grieved at their hardness of heart, and said to the man, "Stretch out your hand." He stretched it out, and his hand was restored. The Pharisees went out, and immediately held counsel with the Herodians against him, how to destroy him.

Mark 3:1–6 (See Matt. 12:9–14; Luke 6:6–11)

"What this man Jesus does not and apparently cannot understand," Yakim reasoned to himself, "is the indispensable role of the law for the chosen people. The law, the torah, is the way for Israel. It is the means of relationship between the nation of Israel and our God, the lamp by which we observe the covenant which the gracious Lord has offered us. Without it there is no light to guide us on the path the Lord of eternity would have us walk. Well did King David say:

> Blessed are those whose way is blameless,
> who walk in the law of the Lord.
> Blessed are those who observe his decrees,
> who seek him with their whole heart,
> Who never do any wrong,
> but always walk in his ways.
> You have laid down your commandments,
> that we should fully keep them.
> (Ps. 119:1–4)

And again he praises the Lord for the gift of his law:

> For ever, O Lord, your word
> is fixed firmly in the heavens.
> Your faithfulness endures through all generations;
> you established the earth, and it abides.

> By your decree these stand fast to this day,
>> for all things are your servants.
> If my delight had not been in your law,
>> I should have perished in my affliction.
>
> (Ps. 119:89–92)

"These last words," Yakim reflected, "apply especially to me. I wish Jesus really comprehended the meaning of these thoughts. I wish the people who seem so attached to his teaching would listen more carefully to the trained teachers of the law. I would gladly share my experience with them. I would tell them how as a young man—despite my careful upbringing and instruction from the teacher Eleazar in this very synagogue, and despite the fact that I had managed to memorize more of the law and the prophets than any of my peers—still I did not understand how the law must come before all else if a man is to begin to know the ways of God.

"It was not a matter of frivolity. I did not, like several of my friends, make light of the detail of the ritual laws simply because they appeared strange by today's standards. While I was far from perfect in my observance of the law, and to my shame and too many times to count did not do all that the law commanded, nonetheless I seriously sought to do God's will. No. My attitude toward the law was far more subtle and far more dangerous.

"I remember now with such gratitude how patient Eleazar was with me. I admired him so deeply, the holiest man I had ever known. If I live to be one hundred I could not begin to emulate his fasting, his almsgiving and prayers, his deep and thoughtful concern, not only for his pupils, but for all who came to him. I shall not presume to judge whether this Jesus is a good son of Israel in his observance of the law and before God. Nor shall I be so foolish as to compare myself with another. But this I do know. Eleazar was a great and holy teacher of God's law, and I do not believe that this Jesus could compare with him in wisdom.

"Nevertheless, when I was young I would keep Eleazar up until late in the night. 'Of course, Yakim,' he would say, 'of course, the law must be interpreted. This is why the good Lord gives to us our understanding, so that we may know how the law applies to our lives. This is our work as teachers: to share the law and the interpretation that has been passed on to us. And where there appears to be some uncertainty and contradiction, then, with much study of all that the law says and with prayers to God for wisdom, we not only may but we must say what we believe the law requires of us.

" 'Two things I bid you never forget, my son. Never tell another that the law asks something of them that you yourself are not willing to seek to observe. And always remember, while the law may at times seem heavy and burdensome to people, it should never be our intent to make it so. The purpose of our interpretation must always be to help the children of Israel follow the will of God.'

"That," I would agree with him, "is precisely my concern. We trust that the will of God is for the good and the ultimate blessing of his people. Must we not, then, when some portion of the law appears in conflict with this good, appeal to a higher principle in the law in order that the law may be fulfilled?"

"Eleazar would smile and sometimes wait for a long time—perhaps hoping that in my heart I would begin to answer my own question. 'In that path,' he said to me, 'much wisdom appears to run. Yet I ask you, my son, whose wisdom is it? Is it not then your wisdom or some other man's wisdom? Does this not then become the highest principle instead of the law of the Lord?'

"Again there was silence which lapsed between us for what seemed like long minutes. Finally he sang me a verse from the great psalm:

> I have more understanding than all my teachers,
>> for your decrees are my study.
>> (Ps. 119:99)

I realized that he wanted me to continue

> I am wiser than the elders,
>> because I observe your commandments.
>> (Ps. 119:100)

"Again there was quiet. I remember now that this was very late in the evening. One could hear the crickets in the summer fields. Then again he sang:

> I will keep your law continually;
> I will keep it for ever and ever.
>> (Ps. 119:44)

I responded

> And I shall walk at liberty,
> because I seek your commandments.
> (Ps. 119:45)

" 'You wish wisdom to be your guide,' the old rabbi said. 'All of the wisdom God intends for his people has been given in the law. No part of it is not of his wisdom. Our work of interpretation is never meant to set any part of that wisdom aside, but to find a way in which all of the law may be observed.

" 'Consider, if you will, other courses. Is each one to decide which law is more important on a particular occasion and which laws need not be observed? In that way lies confusion and chaos. Or, instead, is it the collective agreement of the people that is to say which laws are to be observed and which set aside? Then who is the ruler of the world? Is it not men in place of God?

" 'Someday, my son, I will be gone. There will be no one older here; perhaps not even in Jerusalem. Then they will look to you. Then a young man will come to you seeking better to understand the law. Believe me, you will not on that day want to rely on your own wisdom. Rather you will wish to show him that all wisdom—even though at times this is not clear to us—*all* wisdom is to be discovered in walking in the way of torah.

" 'You must trust in God completely. It is Satan himself, the maker of confusion and foolishness, who whispers to us that one part of the law should be read as higher than another part—that one law contradicts another. Does the Lord God make accidents? Is not the law one, even as the giver of the law is one Lord—blessed be his name? And if we find a way not to observe even one small part of the law, have we not made a question of the whole law?'

"I wanted to try to answer him then—not so much to disagree, but to show him how difficult and steep a matter my studies had revealed this to be. I wanted to offer him actual cases to see whether he could solve them. Yet once more there was stillness. It was as though he had commanded me to silence. It was not just that he was aged and I was young. I was also in awe of his holiness, his austerity. If ever a man loved the law and served the Lord it was this one. Never had I—or have I—known a man to observe the torah so fully. I knew that the Lord was with him.

"Yet, after a time, I yawned. I began to think of other things of life—of my bed, of the next morning. I myself was soon to be given my own first group of younger students. I much looked forward to being a teacher—a rabbi to them.

" 'You want liberty,' Eleazar finally resumed. 'You want to be a man and to decide for yourself what is best. But, tell me, do you truly wish to spend the rest of your days limited and bound by your own ideas of what is good? Would that be freedom?

" 'You know—I do not need to tell you—how you, like me and all others, have not only the good *yetzer,* the good imagination, within you. There is the bad *yetzer* too. You know how it itches you, and you know how subtle it is—telling you what you think you want to believe when the law is in the way of your ease or your passion, or when you would like to please others and earn their favor by setting the law aside for them. Is your idea of liberty continually to be torn between the *yetzer*s? Is not this the affliction from which you desire to escape?

" 'The words of the law may be likened to a medicine of life. They are like a plaster which a king, after he had inflicted a wound upon his son, put upon his wound. He said, "My son, so long as this plaster is on your wound, eat and drink what you like, and wash in cold or warm water, and you will suffer no harm. But if you remove it, you will get a bad boil." So God says to the Israelites, "I created within you the evil *yetzer,* but I created the law as a drug. As long as you occupy yourself with the law, the *yetzer* will not rule over you. But if you do not occupy yourself with the torah, then you will be delivered into the power of the evil *yetzer* and all its activity will be against you." '[1]

"His voice now became very soft and gentle, and it seemed he was as much talking to himself as to me. 'Mercy and truth have met together,' he whispered. 'Righteousness and peace have kissed each other,' I managed to respond (Ps. 85:10). 'This is the Lord's peace for us, Yakim,' he said. 'At times it may seem that the yoke of the law is burdensome. But in time you will come to see that this is the way of the peace that you seek and that in that peace—in utter obedience to God's will—is freedom from the bad *yetzer* and the liberty which God desires for you. You will be free to do all that the law commands you for a blessing upon your own life and all other lives that shall touch yours.'

"Although I was very tired, I went to bed that night with a sense of both exhilaration and peacefulness such as I had never known. My face felt flushed as I lay in bed. I was not so foolish as to believe I could ever after keep the law to perfection. Nor did I dare to think that I might one day be as holy as my beloved Eleazar. But I now knew the path that I would seek to walk. I realized anew that every commandment was a part of a whole, that each fitted together to form one house of the Lord in which I wished always to dwell. As I fell asleep, and again when I woke, I repeated:

> Your decrees are wonderful;
> therefore I obey them with all my heart.
> (Ps. 119:129)

"How good it would be," Yakim continued to reflect, "if Eleazar were still with us—if he were here this very sabbath day. It is not that the people do not listen to me anymore; yet I appear to have so little lasting influence upon their lives. They are so restless, so lacking in the peace which the acceptance of the whole law has brought to my life. They seem ready to give an audience to any teacher that claims to be new and different.

"They once listened to Eleazar, partly because of his holiness and, yes, partly because I and other of his pupils were so faithful to him. Now there is altogether too much disputation, too much disagreement about points of law among Sadducees and Pharisees, this school and that school, and those who call themselves Essenes. Perhaps it is no wonder that the people do not know the difference and are willing to listen to such an uninstructed one as this Jesus, especially since there are some who claim him to be a prophet."

It was not Yakim's job to condemn Jesus or anyone else. Perhaps the man did some good works. There were certainly enough stories about individuals he had healed. "But how easily," Yakim thought, "the people are caught up in sensationalism. How quickly they forget that it is the faithful adherence to the law which brings—not just a temporary healing—but an abiding health, true salvation.

> My eyes shed streams of tears,
> because people do not keep your law.
> (Ps. 119:136)

The mere fact that Jesus may work cures and exorcisms means little in itself. Far more important is the spirit in which they are done. That is the proof of whether or not they are from God. If they are done in order to build up and encourage the covenant with God through obedience to the law, then even he, Yakim, would applaud them. Yet if, as he had heard, they brought the sovereignty of the law into question, then it was his duty both to expose and condemn this false teaching.

It was for this reason that he had made sure his friend Azariah who had the useless, withered hand would be in synagogue today. This would be a kind of test case. The hand had been like this for over ten years.[2] If there was to be an attempted healing, any day of the week would well suffice—any day of the week save the sabbath, when all work, except what was absolutely necessary for the saving of life, was rightly forbidden by the holy law. Any other day he would be delighted if his friend's hand were healed, even if it were only made a little better.

For the moment, however, Yakim bided his time, knowing also that the other teachers who were there would wait for him to take the lead. So far Jesus had not said anything that he regarded as truly dangerous or subversive of what he himself taught the people. And Eleazar had instructed him never to contradict merely for the sake of disputation. He also had to be careful. Those who stood listening were evidently somewhat in awe of the one from Nazareth. Yakim had to confess that even he was not immune to the aura of excitement and new hope the man's words seemed to spread. Yet he remained ready, on guard.

He reminded himself of who this Jesus was. His knowledge of the Scriptures seemed good, but it must also be superficial. He clearly had not been brought up in one of the better synagogues. His approach was often simplistic and paid too little heed to the developments in the better schools. Of what real value was it, for example, when dealing with a question on divorce, to throw the whole issue back on the creation story?[3] One knew, without quoting Genesis, that God had created male and female and ordained that the proper relationship between husband and wife was to be life-long and life-deep, as "one flesh." The controversy came when this relationship was broken, most commonly by adultery. What did the law then permit a man to do with his wife?

And, if Jesus did not know this much, Yakim severely doubted whether he understood what he was talking about when he pretended to know that God was soon to usher in the promised kingdom—that in some ways it was already begun. Oh, yes; Yakim longed for that time as much as anyone. Daily he prayed that the kingdom would come,[4] also recognizing that it was in a sense already here, as he submitted to the rule of God's torah in his heart.[5] Yet that was also what disturbed him; Jesus spoke too little about the importance of torah. He did not deny its role, but neither did he make it clear that the law must be paramount in the relationship between the people and their God. Even in the new age, after all, the torah would continue.

It was easy to talk about new times and a new spirit—to tell little stories about how surprisingly merciful God could be. Soon, Yakim imagined, Jesus would make reference to that often misunderstood prophecy of Jeremiah about the new covenant that would one day be written on the hearts of the people.[6] What was more difficult was to help people understand the kind of obedience that was required—the hours and days and years of steadfast faithfulness—if the law ever were so to become known and God's rule genuinely to be accepted by a sinful nation.

"Oh," Yakim wished again, "if only Eleazar were here now! If I could just see his smile and hear him tell me that I am right." Afterwards they might come together and even joke a little, Eleazar reminding him that he had been foolish to have become so excited about yet another prophet figure. "The woods are full of them," he would say. "They seem to grow wild in Galilee. What harm can one man do to a lifetime of our teaching? You will be here long after he is gone."

And then, once more, Jesus was not all wrong. Yakim urged charity on himself and reminded himself that God had before chosen to speak at least some of his truth through strange and unlikely persons. What Jesus was now saying could not be stated any more forcefully or correctly. Too many people were abusing the law relating to Corban for self-serving ends, and scribes were allowing this, virtually licensing it since this misuse could also be turned to their gain.[7] In such ways did men seek to employ the very word of God for corrupt purposes.

Still, if what he had heard was true, in a more subtle way, Jesus might be guilty of the same corruption. His motives might be said to be of a more spiritual than materialistic character, but all the more dangerous for that. Of course, people would like to think that men might decide when, for what was deemed a good cause, the sabbath law could be set aside. He had heard, for instance, how Jesus had permitted his disciples to pluck ears of grain on the sabbath—countenancing their actions by drawing a far-fetched analogy with King David's eating of the sacred bread in a time of great necessity.[8] How convenient! And once started, how far it could be taken. Soon it would be too difficult—"too dangerous to health"—to prepare the sabbath food ahead of time. Then it would be hard for many people to make the journey to the synagogue. The floodgates would be open. Before long people would be picking and choosing among the commandments, observing only the ones that seemed *beneficial,* and sanctimoniously priding themselves on a virtue that was in reality little more than changing custom and convenience.

Yakim wondered if Jesus might yet be reasonable enough to accept instruction. Once again it was a matter of a relatively untutored individual taking up complex and profound matters and dealing with them simplistically. How true was Eleazar's proverb: "While much knowledge frees a man, a little knowledge enslaves."

It was reported, for instance, that Jesus had attempted to deal with the issue of whether or not healing was permitted on the sabbath by asking, "Which of you, if he has one sheep and it falls into a pit on the sabbath, will not lay hold of it and lift it out? Of how much more value is a human being than a sheep?"[9] On hearing that Yakim did not know whether to laugh or cry. Talk about hackneyed shibboleths! The teachers had discussed that kind of question for years. There was a torrent of oral tradition on the subject.[10] He used those kinds of problems with his beginning students.

It was true that there were some so-called hard-liners on the subject. He had heard that among the Essenes, grouped down by the Dead Sea, there was the kind of rigidity that seemed to develop in little sects. They taught, "Let no beast be helped to give birth on the sabbath day; and, if it falls into a cistern or into a pit, let it not be lifted out on the sabbath."[11] Yet there was so much testimony for interpretation on the other side. In the tradition there were provisions allowing, at the very least, for assistance to animals giving birth on the sabbath, and most certainly to women giving birth.[12] The tradition was clear: "Whenever there is doubt whether life is in danger, this overrides the sabbath."[13]

In fact, there were all sorts of permissive stipulations dealing with emergencies that might arise on the sabbath as well as license for more general human needs and conditions—instructions that allowed frail human beings still to keep the sabbath sacred.[14] In the last analysis Yakim wondered if he would not actually prove to be more lenient and compassionate than Jesus with respect to sabbath traditions.

Now he did not know whether to laugh in derision, or to stamp his foot in anger—as much at the people as at Jesus. Did they think they were hearing something new when he told them, "The sabbath was made for man, not man for the sabbath"?[15] Had Yakim himself not time and again repeated the tradition: "The sabbath is given over to you, not you to the sabbath"?[16] But always when he shared this teaching with them he did so in the context of other careful instruction about the sabbath. The teaching was not intended to permit all manner of activity on the sabbath. Rather was it meant to help toward the understanding that the sabbath commandment was not designed as a burden but as a way of rejoicing. The sabbath and its laws were a gracious gift from God.

This was the point—if they would only listen to him—about which Yakim would like now to remind the people. He wanted to shout at them. They could be so easily misled. The sabbath law and its traditions were not mere customs or secondary teaching. One might well argue that the command to keep the seventh day holy—to sanctify it by doing *no* work—was the cornerstone of the entire torah. Perhaps more than any other law it distinguished the people of Israel from the Gentiles. In this time of confusion and change—of intermixing especially there in Galilee—it was more important than at any other time in Israel's history that the sabbath be kept sacred.

The observance of the sabbath was the most special sign of God's favor and choosing of this people to be his. In revealing the meaning of the sabbath to them he was allowing his chosen ones to share in that creative process in which he himself rested on the seventh day. Into this mystery of the rhythm of creative work and rest Israel was graciously permitted to enter. This never changed. It was as things were from the beginning and are and ever would be. It was the way of the universe—of the sun and moon and all the heavenly lights, ordained by the Lord of eternity who created them all. Blessed be his name forever. Amen.

Yakim closed his eyes as he praised God, and for the moment he kept them shut. He reminded himself that even if only one Israelite understood and held to the sabbath law still that was important. And he was not alone. There were many others, especially in Jerusalem, who kept the sabbath as well as he—probably better. He knew there were pupils of his, standing in this very synagogue, who must also be worried and concerned that the people should give so much attention to this so-called prophet. At least his better students would recognize how much the stability of the whole Jewish society and its relationship with God depended on the traditions that sanctified this day. They and he would not be led astray by a false humanitarianism. Of course, it would be good if Azariah could be made better. But that could happen any other day of the week. There were some things even more important than the healing of a withered hand.

Yakim opened his eyes and was taken aback to find that Jesus' gaze appeared fastened on him, penetrating, as though he were trying to read his thoughts. Even the people at the edge of the crowd grew silent. Out of the corner of his eye Yakim stole a look toward Azariah. Jesus seemed to follow his glance.

Jesus spoke to Azariah: "Come here." Azariah came and stood in the open space before Jesus in the sight of everyone. He appeared frightened. He kept his withered hand tucked in his tunic. Yakim felt his own heart tripping, threatening to miss a beat. Again Jesus looked at him: "Is it lawful on the sabbath to do good or to do harm, to save life or to kill?" This so-called prophet almost glared at him as he said this.

Yakim wanted to answer. He wanted to tell Jesus and the others the things he had just been thinking. But the ramifications were so many, and again Jesus had presented the issue so simplistically. How was one to answer such a loaded question? And Yakim knew he was afraid, fearful that he would be misunderstood—thought to be lacking in compassion. And with his fear there was also a rising anger. Everyone's eyes were upon him, as though he were expected to say something. Jesus seemed almost to be staring him down, as if there were a great contest of wills among them. If only Eleazar were here!

Jesus turned back to Azariah. "Stretch out your hand," he said. Azariah did not move, but neither did his deep-set eyes turn away from Jesus. There was not a sound anywhere in the synagogue. Then from somewhere a child cried, and slowly Azariah took his hand from inside his tunic. Haltingly he reached it out toward Jesus, the fingers seeming to work, groping—for the first time in years seeking to take hold. There was a gasp and then a rising murmur loose in the crowd.

Yakim's eyes were hot. Tears of rage and frustration welled. He did not understand. How could a man heal if he were not of God? Yet how could God be God if he encouraged the breaking of his own sabbath? At the very least this Jesus must have misused this power. It might well take Yakim years of teaching to undo the harm that had been done here this day. Some action would have to be taken to protect the people. He and others would have to take counsel to get rid of this man. In confusion and anger he turned and left the synagogue.

Although we have tried to be sympathetic with Yakim's point of view, we probably cannot help but feel somewhat superior. Long ago we incorporated into our liturgies the great double commandment calling us to love God and our neighbors and then repeating Jesus' words, "On these two commandments depend all the law and the prophets" (Matt. 22:40). Paul advises us similarly: "The one who loves his neighbor has fulfilled the law" (Rom. 13:8). We have also heard the voice of the Lord, interpreted for us by Jesus, speaking through the prophet, "I desire steadfast love and not sacrifice" (Hos. 6:6).[17] Still more succinctly Augustine has written, "Love, and do what you will."[18] While we may appreciate some of Yakim's concerns, his perspective was clearly superseded when Jesus' gospel of love was brought out beyond Judaism. The new gentile Christians were to be a generally law-abiding people, but they were not expected to be obedient to the full complexity of Jewish religious law. Much of that law belonged to a culture different from theirs. Instead, they were expected to heed the basic ethical commandments of the Bible, observe the rightful laws of their own society, and interpret all law by Christian love.[19]

This is how Christians are taught to try to live today, and the debate between Yakim and Jesus likely seems an ancient and rather sterile dispute. Moreover, we regard law itself very differently. There is no longer, as there was in ancient Judaism, one body of law attempting to comprehend much of religious, social, ethical, and criminal law along with determination of contractual and economic relationships and obligations. Instead there are religious and moral precepts that one may choose to observe, and a body of civil or secular law composed and defined through governmental means. Issues are, of course, rarely as clear-cut as we would like them, but we try to keep a distinction between religious and secular law. As vital as secular law is to society, we recognize that its authority is limited to certain areas of human behavior. We do not think of secular law as attempting to embrace the highest principles of life. While some of us may still live in danger of making religious law into a kind of idol and using it to escape opportunities for love and acts of justice, there is no similar danger with respect to the great body of secular laws.

Or so we like to think! Possibly we have come to this consensus not so much by limiting our conception of the scope of secular law as by severely constricting our understanding of religion. Perhaps there are ways in which we have then invested our faith in other directions. Since we are late twentieth-century men and women, let us try to view religion as more than a restricted sphere of ethical matters and questions about God and what happens after death. Let us look more phenomenologically; let us ask where in fact many of us place our highest values. What do we indicate by our actions is most important to us as persons and as a society? What do we believe makes and will preserve us—indeed, save us as a society? What would we fight and even die for?

We would probably like to answer that our ultimate values are to be found in our principles rather than in our system of laws, and that it is these principles that determine our laws rather than the other way around. Yet what are our principles? We may be able to list some of them vaguely (love, justice, life, liberty, and the pursuit of happiness), but, when asked to define them, we often do so in terms of law. And when principle and law come into apparent conflict, how is the issue to be resolved? Surely by law—by building up of more of the law's tradition and application to cover new situations.

Our faith in the law is great. This is especially true for those of us who have obtained some status and position and therefore have a stake in the present social order. We revere our Constitution. It is no accident of language that allows us to speak of our law courts as temples. For many people the most awe-inspiring and hallowed institution in our land is the Supreme Court. More and more often on more and more issues we look to our courts to define for us not only what is legal but what is right. Any distinction grows blurred. A good person is a law-abiding person. Although we may wish to regard Watergate as a gross abnormality, even a United States President becomes an example of a way of life which tries to claim as right what he hoped would not be declared illegal. What is not illegal comes to be regarded as legitimate. Truth becomes what is true according to law.

We may want to maintain that this philosophy is a caricature of our society. Although some thoroughly secular societies, which base their law in a secular philosophy, might invest the law of the state with a kind of religious fervor, we do not—at least most of us do not. Some of us might even like to style ourselves as mildly antigovernment and wary of the litigous tentacles reaching everywhere through our society. Yet the question may still be asked, what would we, when the fabric of our society and our status in it is threatened, defend first? Perhaps with the exception of our lives and the lives of a few close to us, would it not be the system of law that codifies and supports our view of social order? Could we think of anything else more important to defend? Might we not even be ready to bend some of our principles in order to preserve the law's order?

Sadly, however, we are also forced to recognize how readily this same law, which boasts itself to be the ultimate defense of the weak and powerless, can become the bastion for the powerful—so much so that the strength of one's support of the legal system (of "law and order") and insistence that "all are equal before the law" seems to rise proportionately with one's wealth, privilege, or status. Only in recent years have minority and disfranchised groups in society come to recognize more fully that, while the law can be an important weapon for overcoming prejudice and gross inequalities of circumstance and opportunity, it is a double-edged sword. Sooner or later the cries for more equality begin to be cut off by the very precision of legal protectionism. Once made into an idol that might lead us to salvation through the legally perfect human society, the law—which was devised as a basis for human freedom—can become freedom's archenemy. Once more it is seen how sin can act through and use the law to pervert the purposes of the law.

What then is our response? For those whose faith is in the law, the answer is more laws and better laws: laws that are more carefully drawn, and more laws that take individual circumstances into account. Slowly and gradually good legislation and good judges can answer our human problems. Justice will prevail. Society will become better. A good society will make better people.

Yet just as surely it begins to become clear to many of us that the web of the law can never be knitted finely enough. The more tightly it is woven, the more holes there are in it. Something is missing. The law that is meant to save us becomes the net that is strangling our desire for goodness and openness of heart and a genuinely just society. Something is wrong. Paul had a similar experience. "The very commandment which promised life proved to be death to me" (Rom. 7:10).

"Is it lawful on the sabbath . . . to save life or to kill?" On a first reading the question must have sounded like hyperbole. Surely we would prefer Mark's milder form, "to do good or to do harm?" or Matthew's still more reasonable version, "Is it lawful to do good on the sabbath?" (Matt. 12:12). In a similar story Luke puts the question in a way yet better suited for rational debate: "Is it lawful to heal on the sabbath, or not?" (Luke 14:3).[20] But the double structure of the question in Mark's narrative is pressing us beneath the surface to where fundamental life-and-death issues are at stake. The first apposition ("to do good or to do harm?") is strong enough, driving home the realization that the alternative is not just between acting and not acting but between doing good and doing evil by not acting.[21] The second apposition ("to save life or to kill?") then forces us to see that the choice is all the more critical: to heal is to choose the way of life and salvation; not to heal, even in the name of law and religion, is to choose the restricting way that leads to death.

This awareness is firmly underlined by the conclusion of the story as Jesus' antagonists "take counsel" to destroy him. Those very words "take counsel" ominously foreshadow (see Mark 15:1)[22] the last days in Jerusalem, and we recognize again how the healing acts of Jesus have been controversial from the beginning. The story of the man with the withered hand concludes the cycle of stories that began with the healing of the paralytic,[23] and soon Jesus will be charged with doing these things by the power of Beelzebul (Mark 3:22). The challenge he offers to the world's view of religion, ethics, and law is evidently too great to be borne. His healing—his lifesaving acts—will bring about his death, but through his death the new way of salvation will be opened.[24]

Why? Not because Jesus may have been more humanitarian or compassionate. That can always be debated and is not, at least not by itself, a reason for putting a man to death. Nor was it because Jesus made an occasional exception or was presenting his own interpretation of the law. Jesus was calling into question the whole of the law-based orientation toward life. Placing one's faith in law as the principal path toward justice and salvation *in the end* leads not to life but to death.

And the end time—the new time of the kingdom—Jesus believed, was now begun.[25] Jesus commands the man with the withered hand to come and stand before them all. Mark strips the story to its bare essentials and poses the question in its harshest form. The issue cannot be avoided.

Yet, although the matter can be set forth this starkly, it cannot be stated simply, either for Jesus or for ourselves. Jesus' attitude toward the law was evidently complex[26] as was Paul's following him.[27] The law, they maintained, is not bad; it is good. Various forms of law are necessary in any society. To point to the law's limitations does not subvert it but supports it in its proper role and function. While early Christians were accused of being antinomians (people against all law), this was neither Jesus' intention nor Paul's. "Think not," Jesus says, "that I have come to abolish the law and the prophets; I have come not to abolish them but to fulfill them" (Matt. 5:17). Yet, at the same time, "I tell you, unless your righteousness exceeds that of the scribes and Pharisees, you will never enter the kingdom of heaven" (Matt. 5:20). A way must be found to go beyond law as a basis for living and relationship with God and others. The great matters at the heart of life are not bounded by "How will we get by?" or "How will we avoid evil?" but ask, "What will we live for?"

Paul uses the ambiguity of language to reflect this complexity: "Christ is the end of the law" (Rom. 10:4). His ministry at once brings to fulfillment the true purpose of law and ends the belief that law can bring salvation.

Law is good, but it cannot save. Law made into the instrument of salvation becomes the enemy of salvation.[28] The way of law as life's principal guide leads to narrowness and more and more constriction. Again and again Jesus declares to his followers, "You have heard it said . . ." (the law or the law's interpretation says), "but I say to you. . . ."[29] He tells them they must reach beyond and above law to find their positive purposes for living and loving. Law is good, but it cannot provide the motivation and energy that will seek out opportunities to care for others and to heal. Law is good, but it cannot make us free to look for the new tasks God may be calling us to do. The salvation-bearing acts of the coming age fulfill the intention of the law but overflow its borders. Such fresh wine cannot be poured into old wineskins. The wine of the new age is a spirit requiring a new way of life.[30] Security had been found in the limiting horizon of the law, defining the world in which people lived. Jesus was lifting that horizon and offering in the kingdom of God a new way—a new metaphor—for seeing life.

Yakim was an ethical man. Yet Jesus was angry with him because (in what might better be translated as his "blindness of understanding")[31] he was paralyzed into the silent rigidity of the safer and more religious way of the law. Jesus healed the paralyzed Azariah, not just because he was kind, but in order to show that the time for a new way had come.

Yet, before we too easily place ourselves on Jesus' side of this confrontation, we had best reckon again how high are the stakes. Yakim will challenge once more that to attempt Jesus' way is to try to live more in a world that might be than in the world that is. Well could he remind us that the best can become the enemy of the good. Given human limitations and sinfulness, the way of law, whether we see it as religious law or as primarily secular law giving definition to our principles, is far safer. If law is not the final arbiter and absolute—if individuals or groups are given encouragement to set their ideals above the law, we could be subjected to all manner of religious, moral, and political zealotry. Is it not, after all, the genius (perhaps even the divinely sanctioned guardian genius) of the Constitution and Bill of Rights—as further defined by codes of law—which has established in our society the general good above every particular appeal to a higher good? By emboldening people to reach beyond law, Jesus' way could lead to acts of anarchy. The cocoon we call civilization is, after all, thin and fragile. By refusing to grant full primacy to the course of the law his followers could become a danger to the very order and social stability that is the necessary context for ethical behavior.

There is good reason to listen to Yakim. However much we might dream of a world where a passion for true justice and mutual caring would rule, that day, it seems, has not yet come. And at the heart of Jesus' message there is still the threat of revolution to established customs, mores, and laws when these are regarded as the ultimate basis of society. With him, at least some of his disciples, appealing to their hopes for love's justice, liberation, and peace-making, will be seen as endangering law and order. In the end, both Jewish (religious) and Herodian-Roman (civil) law[32] will feel compelled to try to *destroy* that threat with the sentence of death. Jesus will be crucified as an outlaw.

Jesus' teaching with regard to the coming kingdom has been called an "interim ethic."[33] By this expression Albert Schweitzer meant that Jesus' often brief and apparently hyperbolic teaching made sense only if one saw oneself living in the brief interim in history before the final inbreaking of God's reign. In chronological terms Jesus was evidently wrong about the time of that inbreaking, but one should also recognize that, like the prophets before him, Jesus was far more concerned with the present than the historical future. It is into the present that he believed the potential of the kingdom was starting to erupt. Even now the pressure of the advent of God's sovereignty and its demand was time-warping the face of human chronology. Even now one could try to live *as if* the kingdom had begun, standing on the frontier of the kingdom—on the boundary between human reality and divine possibility.

That is how Azariah was healed by Jesus. That is why he could be healed. The paralyzed and desiccated hand that could not reach out is made alive. It now can offer clasps of trust; it can create and caress. It can be touched again. No sabbath law or other law could do this. This was not just another sabbath, but a new day of God's creation. This was the time. For Jesus and for Azariah it was a matter of life or death. And Azariah's healing meant the end of law as the determination of human existence and the beginning of the new way of life.

7 | THE GOOD SAMARITAN

And behold, a lawyer stood up to put him to the test, saying, "Teacher, what shall I do to inherit eternal life?" Jesus said to him, "What is written in the law? How do you read?" And he answered, "You shall love the Lord your God with all your heart, and with all your soul, and with all your strength, and with all your mind; and your neighbor as yourself." And he said to him, "You have answered right; do this, and you will live."

But he, desiring to justify himself, said to Jesus, "And who is my neighbor?" Jesus replied, "A man was going down from Jerusalem to Jericho, and he fell among robbers, who stripped him and beat him, and departed, leaving him half dead. Now by chance a priest was going down that road; and when he saw him he passed by on the other side. So likewise a Levite, when he came to the place and saw him, passed by on the other side. But a Samaritan, as he journeyed, came to where he was; and when he saw him, he had compassion, and went to him and bound up his wounds, pouring on oil and wine; then he set him on his own beast and brought him to an inn, and took care of him. And the next day he took out two denarii and gave them to the innkeeper, saying, 'Take care of him; and whatever more you spend, I will repay you when I come back.' Which of these three, do you think, proved neighbor to the man who fell among the robbers?" He said, "The one who showed mercy on him." And Jesus said to him, "Go and do likewise."

Luke 10:25–37

The parable of the good Samaritan is a story within a story. It is like a jewel mounted in the setting of the dialogue between Jesus and the lawyer. Many careful readers have noticed, however, that the jewel may not quite fit in the setting. The lawyer asks, "Who is my neighbor?" and Jesus responds with a story about a man who acts as an extraordinarily gracious neighbor. The specific question does not seem to be answered, or it is answered only indirectly.

We may also remember that both Mark and Matthew record a similar dialogue between Jesus and a scribe or lawyer (Mark 12:28–31; Matt. 22:34–40) but do not then go on to relate the parable.[1] These observations have led to the suggestion that the parable of the good

85

Samaritan may once have circulated separately in the tradition; perhaps it was told by Jesus on a different occasion.[2] Thus it will be interesting and worthwhile for us to hear it and share in it apart from its present setting or frame story. It will become more clear then who is the central character in the parable. The central figure in most stories is the one with whom everyone else in the story comes into contact. In this story that character is the beaten and injured man.[3]

We are meant to be him in the story. We are to taste his fear, to feel his pain and then his terror at being left, perhaps to die. We can share his desperate consternation when two of his countrymen—two obviously *religious* persons, from whom he had a right to expect help—pass him by. Then we are to feel all his mixed emotions when a stranger, a schismatic, stops to help him.[4]

The Fourth Gospel reflects the distaste and disdain many Jews felt toward Samaritans during this period: "Jews have no dealings with Samaritans" (John 4:9). The Samaritans were despised by the Jews of Judea as at best half-breeds whose religion was a strange mixture of the ancient faith of Israel and idolatries. They were not good people. Yet in the story along comes a Samaritan who is very good. The narrative emphasizes his remarkable goodness.[5]

The story invites us to share in the injured man's confusion and surprise. Should he—could he—let this unclean foreigner help him?

Samuel swore softly to himself. Maybe he should have taken Simeon's advice. His friend, after all, had been down this road several times before. This time of year it was just too hot to travel by day. Several of the ravines had been like ovens.

It would be so good finally to reach Jericho and to put this pack down for the last time. He tried to envision what the town would look like, remembering Simeon's description: There were the palm and balsam trees and houses with their awning porches and windows open to the cool breezes. That's what he wanted above all: to feel those breezes and to drink until he was swimming with the water they said was so plentiful.

Maybe it was his imagination, but he already felt a little cooler. There wasn't that much farther to go and also the sun would be going down in the hills behind him in another hour or so.

And then he might see some fellow travelers. That was the main reason Simeon had advised him to wait. To listen to him, there were robbers everywhere along the road. "The most dangerous road in all of Judea," he had warned. Well, if so, it had been too hot for the thieves too. And despite the heat and the dust and perspiration Samuel was glad he had not waited. It might have been good to have company, but this way he could get his business done in the morning and have the rest of the day for the bazaars and whatever else might come his way. There was this evening too. His energy would return. Jericho was supposed to be full of interesting, even bizarre people. It was said that there were women out on the streets at night. He'd go another two hundred paces before setting the pack down and having one more sip from the gourd.

The pack would be heavier on the return journey with all the goods he was supposed to trade for.[6] He'd need to make his purchases carefully. He hoped that would go all right. He wasn't really very experienced with haggling, and the sellers would probably have strange accents and tricks he had never encountered before. A number of them would be foreigners. He didn't like dealing with them and their unclean ways, but, then, he had a few tricks of his own. He wouldn't let them figure out that this was his first time in Jericho. He wouldn't even buy anything at first, but later, after he had really figured them out, he would get a few presents for himself—and something for his parents too. That would be a way of *honoring* them. He'd give them something for Shabuoth, only a few days away now. They'd be proud of him for a change, and he really would observe the festival this time. At least he wanted to be a devout young man, obedient to the torah and the King of heaven who . . .

He thought he had caught sight of something dark moving behind the boulders ahead. He hesitated, but then went on a bit more slowly. He could feel his heart thumping against his ribs. Maybe he shouldn't have come by himself. There was a sound behind him.

It all happened so suddenly he wasn't sure how many of them there were. They had thrown something over his head and his arms were pinioned to his sides. He wanted to argue, to plead, but he could only try to cry out, his shouts muffled by the heavy cloth, and he began to feel he was suffocating. His pack was ripped away and they were pulling at his clothes.

Then he was down on the hard ground, trying to roll away from the blows. The bastards were kicking him in the ribs—in the groin. Like a rock there was an awful blow against his head. The pain was everywhere, searing, bludgeoning, and then with a blinding stab overwhelming him into darkness.

As a part of him struggled toward a dim and pain-wracked consciousness, another part tried to pull back from it. The hurt as he strove to breathe was renewed violence. The vicious throbbing in his head made every such pain he ever had before seem like a minor headache. There was dust and gravel in his mouth and something warm and wet oozing near his ear.

Only one of his eyes seemed to work and that as in a fog. It was still daylight. Vaguely he wondered how long he had been lying there and then tasted the bile of panic as he was aware of the nearness of death. Would there be anyone to rescue him? He felt himself wretch and vomit without being able to move away from his own puke. Oh savior God, what would become of him? He thought of his mother. Would she ever know? Would anyone come to help him?

He may have passed out again. But now there was a face peering at him. The pain made his vision waver and blur. He tried but failed to cry out, to move his arm. The man was a priest. Samuel could make out the linen sash with its long fringe and the special phylacteries on his arm. Bless the God of the heavens! If only he would now come closer and do something to help him.

He was gone. Gone for help? But why hadn't he stopped? Why hadn't he done or said something to comfort him—him his brother—a brother in need, in terrible need? He would die. He wanted to die, at least to fall back again into unconsciousness—away from the awful pain, now becoming more specific, in his head, his ribs, his groin. He felt sick again.

And then there was another figure, off across the road staring at him. He seemed to be wearing a Levite's prayer shawl. This brother would—must help him. He tried to groan, to move his head. God, the pain! And that one, too, was no longer there. Maybe he had only imagined him. It was a dream before he died. He thought of his sins, all the wrongs he had committed. Was this his punishment and the reason no brother would help him?

But now, bless the King of the Universe, there was a man bending over him, talking to him, scraping the vomit and gravel away from his mouth, then wiping around his eyes, gently moving his head. It hurt so much, but he was so grateful. Help at last.

He tried to respond, to focus on the man's words and tell him how badly he was hurt. *My God! The man was a Samaritan.* It was obvious in his accent and appearance. He was touching him. Samuel was letting himself be touched by him. He could smell the man's strange breath and felt himself recoil at his touch and odd words. Was he really helping him? Was this to be his savior? Was this God's will?

Samuel wanted to speak: to tell the Samaritan he was a Jew; yet he did not want him to go away. He would never be able to tell anyone else about this, but, despite everything he had heard about Samaritans, he needed this man now.[7] He wanted to tell him that, too, even to thank him, if necessary, but, as the man was trying to lift him, all the pain and darkness came flooding back and engulfed him.

Every hearer of the parable of the good Samaritan has at one time or another been the injured man—dealt some cruel and agonizing blow, whether physical or emotional or both.[8] Our life's companion dies. We lose our job or reputation. We are mugged on a dark night or become terrifyingly ill. Depression spread-eagles our spirit. We are fearfully alone. Will we be saved? Can we be saved? Might God's graciousness also come to us by unexpected means? Maybe it will suddenly be present in another whose religious or political views we find deficient and tainted, even intolerable—perhaps a Moonie or a member of the Hare Krishna sect.

The parable asks whether we are able to accept such graciousness. Or perhaps the act of grace happens in any event. We may be so unable to help ourselves that we are not able to prevent it. Having received such goodness from one on whom we had no claim—whose kindness we have in no sense deserved or merited on account of who we are or what we have done—how do we respond? Having experienced the care of one who has no obligation to act as our neighbor, what will be our thoughts when we next see anyone in need? Might we discover a new capacity to empathize with and have compassion upon those whose lives are quite unlike ours? *"Just so,"* observes Dominic Crossan, "does the Kingdom of God break abruptly into a person's consciousness and demand the overturn of prior values, closed options, set judgments and established conclusions."[9]

Now let us return the parable to its setting in Luke's Gospel. It is in that context that it is found, and there are subtle ways in which the dialogue with the lawyer and the parable are closely linked. As we gain insight into their interaction, we may come to believe that a context like this could, after all, have been the original setting for Jesus' telling of the parable.[10]

Our imaginative powers will be stretched by this play within a play. We can see ourselves as the audience watching the lawyer's reactions and observing the other characters as the drama of the good Samaritan unfolds. We may step forward ourselves to play the part of the lawyer. We are then asked to be ourselves being the lawyer being the injured man—seeing through his eyes the priest, the Levite, and the Samaritan, while also trying to imagine their feelings. We are also asked to be ourselves being the lawyer acting in the parts of the priest, the Levite, and the Samaritan. We are pulled well out of ourselves into the lives of others. Then suddenly, when the whole story is over, we will be just ourselves again, trying to interpret in the stories of our lives what we have experienced. The story within a story is of particular interest to us because it tells not only of one who is healed but of one who heals, while it also helps us to perceive how such healing can happen.

A lawyer stands up to ask Jesus a question. We are told little more about him, but are meant to understand that he would have been regarded as a kind of teacher, an expert in his knowledge of the law of Moses along with the other traditions and their interpretations. We remember again that at that time there would have been no sharp distinctions made between what we might think of as religious law and civil law. The whole of the law spoke not only to what Jews were required to do and not to do in society, but set out before them what ought to be done if one were to fulfill all God's will for his people.

This lawyer, we are led to believe, has more in mind than an interesting discussion. He intends to *test* Jesus.[11] Although we can only speculate on his motives, the suggestion is certainly present that he would like to sound Jesus out. While the lawyer's opening question does not specifically ask about Jesus' understanding of the law, that would have been the context and presupposition of the initial inquiry. Perhaps he wanted to show that Jesus was unlearned, insufficiently trained in knowledge of the law and methods of argumentation and application, and so discredit him as a legitimate teacher of the people of the torah.

Perhaps he hoped to diminish Jesus' influence by creating an opportunity for him to displease one segment or another of Jewish society. It is like the game that is regularly played in our time with presidential candidates. The candidate doesn't wish to become too specific before he must, while reporters ask questions like, "What are your priorities?" "What are the most important issues?" By putting a concern with inflation before jobs or environmental matters before stimulation to the economy, the candidate is likely to lose influence with those who give vigorous emphasis to what were mentioned as secondary matters.

The lawyer's question sets out a big net and invites Jesus to become entrammeled in it. "Teacher," he asks (perhaps with a note of condescension in his voice), "what must I do to inherit eternal life?"[12] For the lawyer, this is another way of asking which are the most important features in all the law.

Jesus shows himself adept at this form of testing debate. Since the lawyer has put the question in personal terms, Jesus turns the question back to him: "What is written in the law? How do *you* interpret?"

There is, however, now more going on than rabbinic gamesmanship. Jesus has altered the tone of the discussion. By assuming the lawyer's personal concern, Jesus has considerably deepened his involvement. The lawyer's question is heard as a way of expressing the heart of human longing: "What do you feel to be the true and enduring meaning of life? Which are the purposes and values that are everlasting?"

The lawyer gives an excellent answer. Although not definitively codified as such at the time, this double commandment represents the highest aspirations of Jewish life and summarizes the spirit that undergirds all ethical issues.[13] "You shall love the Lord your God with all your heart, and with all your soul, and with all your strength, and with all your mind; and your neighbor as yourself." As far as putting it into words is concerned, it could not be said any better. "You have answered quite rightly," Jesus responds. "Do this and life is yours."

Presumably they could have left the discussion there, but as both the lawyer and Jesus realized, this summary of law led directly to the next and more practical question. How does one *do* this? Here is the challenge. How can one attempt to enact such lofty ideals?

The lawyer seeks a way to frame this practical concern and also to put the pressure back on Jesus. We are told, in addition, that he now feels the need to justify himself—to demonstrate that he knew he was posing no simple or quickly answered issue when he asked about gaining eternal life. It is difficult enough to know how we are to love God, but this love is at least more easily claimed since it is so hard to evaluate. One can maintain that one loves God, but amid the exigencies and ambiguities of daily life it is far more difficult to show that one loves one's neighbors.

We may suspect as well that the lawyer has been caught up in the personal participation that Jesus invited. The lawyer wants to know about values that both transcend and give meaning to life. He also shares with others the need to rationalize and justify his behavior. How can I love others as myself? To begin with, "Who is my neighbor?"

Jesus now reveals his power of insight and deep pastoral concern. We have seen that the parable of the good Samaritan does not appear directly to answer the lawyer's question. But Jesus has heard the question behind the question. He recognizes that out of his need to justify himself the lawyer is really asking the opposite of what he seems to ask. His is not a positive concern—wanting to know who it is that he might reach out to and love. The lawyer's real question is, "Who is *not* my neighbor?"

Again we are invited to be the lawyer. His real question is a question we all feel forced upon us. Think of the daily demands that other people are ready to make on our limited resources of time, energy, and money. Whom can we exclude from our neighborly care while still maintaining a clean conscience?

Every day I meet people who want at least a little bit of my attention and sometimes my money. In my present work I have relationships with students, faculty, staff, trustees, friends, graduates, benefactors. I may be encountered by panhandlers whose lives seem wasted. Now and then, with a good night's sleep and someone's pat on the back, I might dare to feel I can manage it all. But most days I realize I would be overwhelmed if I tried to share myself or my worldly possessions with all these people. And if I did and others heard about it, there might be no end to the stream at my door.

And beyond them, what about all the others? The hundreds of thousands, the millions? I see their empty stares in the newspapers and on television. How many of them starve to death every year? How many will lead impaired lives just because they will not receive basic nutrients during the first few months of their existence? I cannot help all of them—hardly even a few of them.

Yet I do not want to go around every day and all day feeling guilty. Yes! Lines do need to be drawn. And this is the role of law: to help me understand ethical definitions. Whom can I set outside the limits of my neighborly concern without forfeiting my claim to be an ethical person?

Jesus, as he so often does, responds with a story. The method reminds us that it is in life itself—in the actual circumstances of daily living—that the questions become most real and we may begin to glimpse the possibility of God's presence in the world.

A man was going down the steep hilly road from Jerusalem to Jericho. Alone on the road he was easy prey for robbers who took everything he had, even his clothes. As muggers will, out of an overspill of their own anger and self-hatred, they beat him severely and left him half-dead by the roadside.

Now two supposedly ethical people came by. Since many of us are religious people, we should note that in their roles they are very religious too. It would be a mistake, however, to think that the lawyer's question belongs only to self-styled religious folk. It comes from everyone who is concerned to justify himself or herself.

The ethical people—a priest and a Levite (an individual who would have had hereditary privileges and functions in the temple)—passed by without stopping. From time to time hearers of the story have been interested to speculate about why they did. There is no reason to believe that they were not good men, and it is not hard to invent creditable moral reasons. Maybe they were hurrying to their temple duties which they regarded as ultimately more significant than helping a single injured person. The injured, the poor, and the sick would always be in the world, but the praise of the Creator and Sustainer of all things living must never cease. Unless there is worship of that which is greater than self, men and women would not be able to continue on and find the strength to help one another. Or they may have thought that the man was dead and were concerned that by touching him they would make themselves legally unclean and so unfit for their responsibilities.[14] It is not inconceivable that they knew of someone even more desperately ill—perhaps a friend or relative—whom they felt had a greater claim upon their help.

We should probably reckon with the most likely possibility, that they were afraid. I would have been. I have passed by people lying on the sidewalks in the slum areas of our cities. Maybe they were drunk or dead. I was afraid to become involved. It was a job for the police.

And maybe it was a ruse. Out there on a lonely road—maybe that was how the robbers tricked you into stopping. And then, when you bent over, the man on the ground grabbed you and others jumped out of the bushes, and *wump* on the back of the head! Then you would be the man in the ditch! Better to find some other neighbors to love, try to forget this one, and make up for it by being extra kind to someone else.

A reminder of how slow we should be to judge the priest and the Levite is to be found in an experiment used on a number of seminary students.[15] It was one of those little exercises that graduate students in psychology love to conduct. The seminary students were divided into three groups and asked to come for individual interviews. After this session they were then asked to cross over to another building for a second interview. Lying in an alley between the buildings was a man. As the students would cross the alley this man would groan and generally indicate his distress.

The results of the experiment indicated only one discernible factor in determining whether the students would make any real effort to help the man. It was not how charitable, kind, or generous of spirit individual students were thought to be. The significant factor was how much time they were led to believe they had between interviews. One group was instructed that they were late and should hurry, the second was simply told to go directly over to the other building, and the third was informed that there might be a wait between interviews. It was mainly students in the last group who acted like "good seminarians" and were inclined to see if something could be done for the man.

In Jesus' parable we are not given many details about the third individual to come down the Jerusalem-Jericho road. What we are surely intended to notice, however, is that he was a Samaritan. There in the heart of Judea this foreigner certainly had cause to maintain, "This is no neighbor of mine."

Yet it is the Samaritan who has compassion. If the injured Judean was to be considered his enemy, the Samaritan exemplifies Jesus' bidding that the disciples' love is to emulate the love of God ("You have heard that it was said, 'You shall love your neighbor and hate your enemy.' But I say to you, Love your enemies" Matt. 5:43–44).[16] He interrupts his own journey in order to bind up the man's wounds, using wine to cleanse and oil as balm. He puts him on his mount and takes him to an inn. There he ensures his care for however long it will take him to become well.

At this point we return to the frame story where we are meant to share in the lawyer's response as Jesus asks, "Which of these three, does it seem to you, showed himself a neighbor to the man who fell among the robbers?" "The one who showed mercy on him," the lawyer replies. Jesus closes the conversation by saying to the lawyer, "Go and do likewise."

How well had Jesus met the lawyer's concern? The lawyer, we remember, had really been asking, "Who is not my neighbor? Whom can I not treat with neighbor-love while still managing to see myself as a law-fulfilling and respectable person?"

More than this, he also wanted Jesus or the law—someone or something else—to answer his question for him. While on the surface it might appear that Jesus was shifting the grounds of the discussion, at a deeper level he really was insisting that the subject stay the same, in both senses. The question belonged to the one who asked it, and the real focus of concern was with whether and how law might provide limiting definitions for ethical behavior. Jesus' response by way of parable puts another question to all who are that lawyer. His story allows the lawyer to be in the position of an injured man who was graciously befriended by someone who had no reason to help him but who evidently did not have to ask the lawyer's question. "What does that now do to your understanding of why you would help another? And why," we are effectively asked, "do you need to know who is or is not your neighbor?

What does your asking of this question tell you about your reasons for caring for others? Why are you not content to help those you find you can help and leave it at that?"

Our response, of course, is that we cannot leave it at that, for our anxious insecurity prompts us to keep trying to shore up our slipping sense of moral worth. Continually we strive to define and limit situations, interpreting life by law. Since we cannot help everyone, we want definitions that will tell us whom we can legitimately set outside our concerns. This is what ethical law is for! This is what religion is all about—to help us escape our guilt feelings. And into that losing struggle goes so much of the energy that might have been used to embrace our own humanity and to reach out to others.

For the disciples, much of the power of the parable of the good Samaritan came from their awareness that Jesus did not just tell this story. He stood in and behind it. In one role he is the beaten and friendless man (he who himself will be crucified) whose need calls to those who pass by, offering them the opportunity to give a neighbor's care. "Lord, when was it that we saw you hungry and fed you, or thirsty and gave you drink, a stranger and took you home, or naked and clothed you? When did we see you ill or in prison and come to visit you?" "As you did it to one of the least of mine, you did it to me" (Matt. 25:37–40). In another role in his followers' memory and experience, Jesus is himself the one who stops to help; he is the unexpected good Samaritan to Nathan, Jonathan, Legion, Zacchaeus, the Syrophoenician woman, Azariah, Bartimaeus, Mary Magdalene, and so many others. And then in a sense he is both the injured and the helping man; he is the wounded healer who is able to come to the aid of others because he knows their hurt.

But, no; he could not help everyone either. And there were times, we are told, when he was tired and when he went up to the hillsides by himself to pray. He could not love others if he did not have care and love for himself. Yet doubtless there were a number of people who had come to him who went home disappointed.

Evidently he did not have to ask the lawyer's question. The power of his ministry emanated from a deep awareness that he was already included in the acceptance and care of God. This was not a care he had to earn by moral action. He was free from the need to justify himself so that his energy was released for the people he could help. He reached out to them from a stance unencumbered by a need to use his help of them as a means for bolstering his own sense of self-worth. This power healed people.

The lawyer had expressed well what we are meant to do. We are to love the Lord our God with all our heart, soul, strength, and mind; and our neighbors as ourselves. Having been graciously helped—apart from any question of whether we had some claim upon this grace—we are enabled to be graceful to others. It is in responding to the love of God offered to us that we may come to know that we really are lovable and loved and then love-able, enabled to love. Finding the love of ourselves, we discover the freedom to reach out to others without needing to prove that we are good and worth love. Having been healed, we can be healers. And as we do love others we discover the mystery that in them we are also loving the God in whom they have their being, in whose image they are made, and whose love can likewise reach through them to us. The double commandment is integrated into one great commandment of love.

Not only do we learn that we are to love God and our neighbor but we begin to learn how this can be done. The four-times repeated use of the word *do* in our story ("what shall I do to inherit eternal life?"; "do this and you will live"; "the one who did mercy"; "do likewise") now assumes its full force. From this perspective the entire gospel message unfolds in the exchange between the lawyer and Jesus. We have moved beyond speculation and interpretation on the subject of neighborliness. Freedom for a new kind of life and a new relationship with God and one's neighbors is offered to the lawyer and to us. Our deepest problem, we remember, is not that we do not know what to do. Our problem is that we cannot find the power to do it. The hearing of the parable offers us that power. We, too, can do healing like the Samaritan.

Yet the parable threatens to unnerve us even as it exhilarates us. Do we dare to be . . . do we even want to be this free? All of us have known moments when we have felt this power and freedom, when we have ventured beyond our comfortable boundaries toward that frontier where Jesus proclaimed the kingdom of God to be breaking in. We have realized what it can mean to stop trying to be merely ethical (observers of the law) and to start being good—to allow a positive love rather than a defensive concern with morality to be our guide. We begin to sense what Jesus meant when he insisted that "unless your righteousness exceeds that of the scribes and Pharisees, you will never enter the kingdom of heaven" (Matt. 5:20). But we have also seen ourselves shrinking back.

We now realize just how well Jesus had heard the initial question: "What must I do to inherit eternal life?" By his questions and our answers he has led us to that arena where our deep desire to stretch the borders of self and to reach out is fiercely guarded by a fearful anxiety, which wills to maintain and fortify its defenses at all costs. In the midst of that struggle we have been told of one who found life beyond those fortifications and we have been shown something of the road that he walked, looking for those he might love.[17]

8 | BARTIMAEUS

And they came to Jericho; and as he was leaving Jericho with his disciples and a great multitude, Bartimaeus, a blind beggar, the son of Timaeus, was sitting by the roadside. And when he heard that it was Jesus of Nazareth, he began to cry out and say, "Jesus, Son of David, have mercy on me!" And many rebuked him, telling him to be silent; but he cried out all the more, "Son of David, have mercy on me!" And Jesus stopped and said, "Call him." And they called the blind man, saying to him, "Take heart; rise, he is calling you." And throwing off his mantle he sprang up and came to Jesus. And Jesus said to him, "What do you want me to do for you?" And the blind man said to him, "Master, let me receive my sight." And Jesus said to him, "Go your way; your faith has made you well." And immediately he received his sight and followed him on the way.

Mark 10:46–52 (See Matt. 20:29–34; Luke 18:35–43)

The Gospel stories are full of surprises, not the least of which are the people who now claim to put their faith in Jesus: the man who once could not talk, another who was crazy, the foreigner who insists the Lord healed her daughter, the head of the local tax office. Somehow one would expect to pick up the Gospels and find there, for the most part, good common sense. Instead there are unexpected occurrences and often outlandish parables—holy jokes right at the heart of the good news. Jesus describes a splendid dinner party which the invited guests did not attend because they were too busy with their affairs (Luke 14:15–24; Matt. 22:1–10). Instead it was the poor, the blind, and the lame—the outcast and riffraff of the city—who sat around in their rags, the amputees with their wooden legs propped up on pillowed chairs feeding delicacies to the blind. In a world where it was often assumed that wealth and status were signs of God's approval and illness and poverty of divine disfavor, striking reversals take place. In the kingdom things do not work out the way one might expect. Impossible things happen to improbable people. We are offered a new orientation, a new way of seeing life's possibilities. But, if we are truly to see, we must first be disoriented.[1] We must experience the *metanoia,* the change of heart

99

and mind—the repentance, made possible and demanded by the advent of the kingdom of God.

A kind of riddling goes on. How do the last become first and the first last? How does one lose one's life and find it? How can a person have ears and not hear or eyes and not see? How are the deaf able to hear and the blind to see? Frequently these challenges come in the form of stories, both haunting and comic, which twist and turn in ways that make cracks in our shallow readings of the meaning of life. In the parables Jesus told and in the parables he enacted we hear at once of stern judgment and amazing grace in such a manner that we find ourselves standing on unsettling ground. Through the cracks we are able to glimpse fundamental depths where the nature and purpose of our lives are brought radically into question, but where we may also catch sight of the foundation of all hope. Such is the character of the story Mark presents when he tells us of Bartimaeus, the blind beggar.

The story takes place at a pivotal point in the Gospel. It is the last of the healings and has been artfully prepared for. It has been described as a coda[2] about the meaning of discipleship, following as it does a long section in the middle of the Gospel which also begins with the healing of a blind man (Mark 8:22–26). Between these two healings we hear of the struggles of disciples to *perceive* what it means to follow Jesus.[3]

Previous to this section we have been introduced to religious leaders whom one would normally regard as having very good sight. These officials were among the best educated men of their time. They were trained in the reading and interpretation of the scriptures. Their prayer and religious devotion would have put most of us to shame. Many of them would have felt they had gained special insight into God's purposes. Yet, they could not see Jesus as anything other than a threat to their understanding of how God related to the world. John's Gospel repeatedly underscores this irony. Jesus was the light of the world.

> He was in the world; but the world, though it owed its being to him, did not recognize him. He came to his own people, and they did not receive him.
> (John 1:10–11)

After the Fourth Gospel version of the healing of a blind man, Jesus says: "It is for judgment I have come into the world—to give sight to the sightless and to make blind those who see" (John 9:39).

For a time, Jesus' disciples do begin to perceive how God was present in his ministry and person. Peter glimpsed this for a moment and confessed Jesus to be the Christ, the expected one from God. But then he cannot understand how God would be acting in Jesus as the Son of man who will suffer and be killed.

Together with James and John on the mount of the transfiguration Peter again caught sight of the possibility that it was through and in Jesus' very humanity that God had chosen to signal his presence. Yet, once more, the mystery becomes opaque and before long the disciples grow fearful and resort to arguing among themselves about which of them is the greatest. Still later in the narrative James and John, when asked the same question that Jesus will ask of Bartimaeus ("What do you want me to do for you?" [Mark 10:36]),[4] respond with a request that one of them sit at his right hand and the other at his left in his time of glory. By seeking to interpret their association with Jesus as a matter of privilege and their special deserving they too have become blind. They also have eyes but do not see well.

Jesus, who "on the way"[5] to Jerusalem has already alarmed his disciples with teachings about his suffering as the Son of man, tries once more to instruct them. The way of love, with all its joys, yet inescapably involves opening the self to compassion and sorrow. One cannot love without seeing the pain of others and being exposed to the grief they will cause. "Are you able to drink the cup that I drink or be baptized with the baptism with which I am baptized?" (Mark 10:38). The two disciples claim that they can, but the incident causes the others to become indignant with James and John. Jesus appeals to all of them:

> You know that in the world the recognized rulers lord it over their subjects, and their great men make them feel the weight of authority. That is not the way with you; among you, whoever wants to be great must be your servant, and whoever wants to be first must be the willing slave of all. For even the Son of man did not come to be served but to serve, and to give his life as a ransom for many.
>
> (Mark 10:42–45)

But who is able to perceive and follow in faith such a Son of man as the one who can heal and save the world?

It is at this point that the evangelist brings Jesus and his little band of uncertain followers to the town of Jericho.[6] Immediately ahead awaits an obscure but already ominous encounter in Jerusalem. All around them now is tumult. An excited crowd wants to catch sight of Jesus—to look him over and perhaps hear him—to see if they can make anything of him. The disciples are tired, fearful, wishing they had never left Galilee. Jesus, however, is determined. He presses on through Jericho.

Just beyond the gate of the town there sits a blind beggar. The story provides us his name.[7] We are given little other information, although one can imagine many such figures sitting by the city's gates.[8] The travelers through Jericho were numerous, many of them having come on long journeys to barter or sell their goods. Some would be feeling expansive as they left. They might throw a coin in the direction of the beggar's outspread cloak and perhaps chuckle as he groped after it. For all but the most cunning and skillful of beggars, however, even their best income resulted in little more than a starvation diet in the midst of an uncomfortable life. The days began in a damp chill that often mounted toward sunburnt and dusty afternoons. For one who could not see, there was not even the dull attraction of watching the passers-by.

Doubtless many would have grown lethargic sitting there day after day. Idle conversation and any desire for banter would have died as the sun rose high. On most days sleep became a welcome companion. Sightless life held little interest. Asleep or awake, the blind beggars hung down their heads.

There are, however, blind people whose other senses grow more acute, who surprise us by intuiting from smells and sounds that which escapes our sight. They can hear a conversation with better insight than many of us. One is led to believe that Bartimaeus might have been such a man.

This happened to be an unusually cold morning, and he sat huddled with his threadbare cloak around him, leaving only the corners unfolded in the hope that someone might toss him a coin. He sensed the commotion before he heard it, a tension and note of expectancy in the air—and then the voices telling of Jesus of Nazareth, the prophet and healer, who was soon to pass by.

A crowd two and three deep had pushed its way between him and the road. Voices now grew louder, conversation more excited: Jesus and his group were drawing closer. Bartimaeus felt a sudden urge to call out, to ask for help. But he did not know how one was supposed to address this Jesus, what title of honor to offer. When he sensed that the prophet had drawn nearly opposite him on the roadway, he shouted out, "Jesus, Son of David, have mercy on me."

The evangelist seems to suggest that the designation Son of David was both right and yet not right for Jesus, perhaps playing on the irony that Bartimaeus could perceive but not yet fully see.[9] Yes, Jesus was the one whom God had chosen to fulfill the ancient promises—who was soon to be hailed as king of his holy city. He was bringing to pass the prophecies of healing of the messianic age to come. Yet it was not a claim to be messiah because of Davidic descent that most characterized Jesus' mission. He was not about to establish a new kingdom by means of worldly power. He was a different kind of messiah.

In any case, the beggar was creating a disturbance. Jesus must have had more important concerns than this blind man; more vital matters were imminently at stake. Voices hissed at him. Someone turned and rudely told him to "shut up."

Bartimaeus felt fear twitch in his facial muscles, but neither could he quiet the upsurge of hope welling from deep within him. No, he did not know what to call him, but he knew what the designation meant to him. It meant, *You are the promised one of God—the one that God sends to heal his people and give them vision—the one I pin my hopes on.* With an intensity that focused all his senses he saw this Jesus as the one who could help him. From the vantage of his heightened hope he looked toward Jesus and beheld him as others did not. Still more loudly he cried out, "Son of David, have mercy upon me!"

The prophet stopped in his own profound journey. Some of the crowd considered that he might show his charity by giving the man a coin. Others thought he would chastise the blind fool for using the Davidic title in so loose and dangerous a fashion. That kind of talk could get a man crucified.

"Call him," he said.

Those nearest to Bartimaeus turned to him. "Take heart; rise, he is calling you."

Bartimaeus threw aside his cloak—the few small coins he had left out as incentives bounced away on the hard clay. He jumped to his feet and groped his way from arm to arm in the direction of Jesus' voice.

"What do you want me to do for you?" Jesus asked.

"Master, let me see again."

"Your faith has made you well."

Immediately, we are told, Bartimaeus received his sight and followed Jesus "on the way."

Clearly the evangelist means this to be a paradigm or master story about how one comes to true discipleship.[10] How is it, we are forced to ask, that the great religious leaders of the time had become so myopic that they were blinded to God's presence in Jesus? How is it that the disciples in their own fashion had also become dull of eye? The implications are inescapable: those who pride themselves on their own vision and believe they perceive what is of importance in the world can become so shortsighted and narrow of perspective that they render themselves blind to that which is of the essence. In their pursuit of what they think they deserve in life they lose sight of what they truly need. Nor can they see that the road to salvation must lead through humility and suffering; love's glory requires love's passion for others.

In contrast, Bartimaeus brings to Jesus (in Calvin's phrase) "nothing but the begging." Persistently beseeching Jesus out of his great need and hope, Bartimaeus has pure faith in the Lord's healing as a gift of God's love and justice. This will be for him a sign that the messiah has come and the new age begun. And the gift brings him the vision he needs to follow (*akolouthein*, from which the word *acolyte*) Jesus "on the way" to Jerusalem, to Calvary, and to the new life of salvation.[11] The Greek word *sōzein*, we recall, means both "healing" and "salvation." It is a fulfillment of the prophet's promise:

> And I will lead the blind
>   in a way that they know not;
> In paths that they have not known
>   I will guide them.
> I will turn the darkness before them into light
>   the rough places into level ground.
>
> (Isa. 42:16)

In its context, Bartimaeus's story, we recognize, presages Paul's story—the story of a man who thought he had a superior view of God's will, until the day he was made blind, but then was given the vision of who Jesus was for him and for the world. The sonship and sense of acceptance that Paul had ardently wanted with God were not to be gained through his bogus righteousness—the claims he could make by birth and upbringing or by instruction and religious zeal. The relationship of love could only be discovered as a gift.[12] But this gift Paul could see only after being made blind. Together with Bartimaeus and many another disciple Paul could then sing:

> Amazing grace, how sweet the sound
> That saved a wretch like me.
> I once was lost, but now am found,
> Was blind, but now I see.

Also with Bartimaeus, Paul not only sees Jesus as his savior, but also receives a vision of the way ahead. For Paul this includes a vision of the future Christian community. Again it is no easy road. Controversy, suffering, and passion are part of the journey. Cherished understandings of how one becomes a disciple and what is essential to relationship with God will be challenged and changed. But Paul is now determined to try to preach nothing other than Christ crucified and risen and not to allow human mores and traditions to become a bar to discipleship and the full acceptance of others—Jews and Greeks, slaves and free, male and female—into Christian community.

Other disciples live their own forms of the story. In the dark night before Jesus' crucifixion, Peter denies his Lord. Even after the vision of the resurrection he experiences painful difficulty in accepting the opening of the kingdom to Gentiles. He resists, starts to go forward, and then balks. He finds it particularly hard, because of Jewish dietary restrictions, to allow Jewish and gentile Christians to eat at the same table. God then brings upon him the darkness of a trance and shows him a vision that enables him to set aside all such restrictions for the sake of the gospel (Acts 10:9–16; 11:1–18).

Other versions of the story have been experienced in the lives of saints and mystics and many men and women of faith. There is a time—for most of us there may be several times—when one feels enshrouded in what has been called "The Cloud of Unknowing." While this cloud may form at the beginning of the religious quest, it often forms when one is far advanced and finds (perhaps finds again) that unaided reason and human efforts cannot achieve nearness to God. The cloud may especially descend when we have imagined that our relationship with God is a matter of our learning, our way of seeing, our morality, the certainty of belief we profess, or hours spent in prayer. Then for long periods (perhaps in some sense throughout life's search) there may well come "The Dark Night of the Soul" when one can only try to walk by what Saint John of the Cross describes as "dark and pure faith"[13]—when the soul is led "by the most lofty path of dark contemplation and aridity, wherein it seems to be lost."[14] The relationship and vision one longs for can come through that cloud and in that night only as a pure gift from God.

This imagery of cloud and darkness has often been regarded with suspicion. Critics see the dangers of an irrationalism and anti-intellectualism which periodically infiltrate and distort Christian faith and practice. Rightly they remind us that Christians are bade to love God with the whole self-mind as well as heart and soul.

But the experience of those who have been found by God in darkness does not represent an appeal against reason. Rather is it a recognition of the proper role that reason and human effort have in the discovery that both life itself and its Giver are gifts. Often a form of blindness can be the only way of making individuals let go of their own way of insisting on seeing in order that there can be true vision.[15] Reason may direct a person toward encounter with God and help to interpret the sense of God's presence, but reason alone cannot form the vision.

The vision is a gift of love. If it were otherwise—if, for example, it were through our intellectual efforts that we could *comprehend* God, then our encounter would be with our idea (our image) of God and not with God as he is. We would be attempting to take God into our understanding and relate to him as we do finite objects and persons who are distinct from ourselves. But God is the source of life from whose being comes our existence and in and through whose life we exist. It is only when we experience his love and reach out in response that we begin to perceive the life of God and who we may be in relationship to him. According to Thomas Aquinas it is only when moved by love that we may find what is beyond knowing.[16] In the words of the author of *The Cloud of Unknowing*, "Only to our intellect is God incomprehensible, not to our love."[17] This relationship, we realize again, is made possible not by our initial endeavors but by the gift of God's Spirit enabling us to do what otherwise we could not. "We love because he first loved us" (1 John 4:19).

We all have our own stories of darkness and light. Probably at some time each of us has been given a form of new sight. Having received vision like Bartimaeus, we may have been surprised and alarmed first to see, looming before all else, the way to Jerusalem and the cross. Still we treasured the gift of our sight as we tried to follow on the way—seeing the world's need for compassion through God's eyes. Sooner or later, however, something happened to blur our vision. We may have yielded to the temptation to try to interpret the gift as, at least in part, a reward for our own intellectual efforts or religious strivings. Perhaps we became like the Galatians to whom Paul wrote in simmering frustration.

> O foolish Galatians! Who has bewitched you, before whose eyes Jesus Christ was openly portrayed as crucified? Let me ask you only this: Did you receive the Spirit by works of the law, or by hearing with faith?
> (Gal. 3:1–2)

Or maybe we just began to experience all the steep hills and deep valleys on the way. The road of compassion became arduous, painful, and then frightening. We preferred our discussions about love to love's actions. It seemed more attractive to beautify and decorate our vision of the passionate Jesus—only to find that it had faded. It ceased to be a window to God and became instead a painting we hang upon our wall. It no longer had light of its own, and after a time we could not see what gave us insight. We knelt and prayed before it, but all grew dark once more. Again we found ourselves beggars with nothing to offer, sitting outside the gates of the city in our own world of night—waiting and hoping for Jesus to pass by.

We may find that the story happens over and over again. Although there is no set periodicity, I experience a kind of gyration in my life. I turn from times of warmth and light to twilight and then darkness. All the wrong in me and evil in the world spreads a pervasive gloom of despair. "Darkness is my only companion" (Ps. 88:18).

There was a time when I became somewhat frantic in that darkness, alternating between being ready to declare my loss of faith dramatically to some shocked council of clergy and being anxious to race back to my room to read yet another book about God and jerk the wheel of prayer. But God is absent from mantra and meditation. He is not to be found in philosophy or theology. He cannot be conjured up by liturgy, no matter how ancient or contemporary. He is not present in institutions; creeds convey no sense of him. The scriptures tell tales of long ago in another land.

Finally I have learned that in the night there is little I can do but huddle and wait. Sometimes the darkness seems endless, so cold that the breath of my wordless prayers is but a vapor. I try to remember the poet's words:

> I said to my soul be still, and let the dark come upon you
>   Which shall be the darkness of God. . . .
> . . . .
> In order to arrive at what you do not know
>   You must go by a way which is the way of ignorance.
> In order to possess what you do not possess
>   You must go by the way of dispossession.
> In order to arrive at what you are not
>   You must go through the way in which you are not.
> And what you do not know is the only thing you know.[18]

And then, miraculously, once more the daystar rises and life returns. Perhaps on a day of least expectation I hear that Jesus of Nazareth is passing by. I cry out in desperate need, in hope wanting to be faith,[19] "Jesus Son of David, *whoever you are,* have mercy on me." Voices rebuke: "The Lord can't pay attention to your kind of need." But I cry out all the more.

He stops. "What do you want me to do for you?"

"Master, let me see again."

What happens is a miracle because it is not what I manage to make myself believe. I laugh because it is so improbable and so graceful. It is what seems to happen to my sight even in the face of my sins and in the face of friends dying, of the children whom I have watched in hospitals turning on a spit of pain—and of the millions starving. But I see God in Jesus and in others caring, and he wants me to care. And I discern purpose in the caring.

The light I see is never perfect. Always there are clouds, some rain. Yet then I have come to recognize that the night is never pitch darkness either. As one's eyes become accustomed, there are traces of last evening and then the beginning of the dawn. Even in the middle of the night one can discern remembered shapes. I have begun to learn that I can wait there. I need not be terrified of the dark. I begin to see that I must experience the dark if I am to know the day—that doubt need not be faith's foe, but a way of purifying vision of that which is not of love. The night too can be a gift—a time of learning and relearning the need for love. This can be "the dark night, through which the soul passes in order to attain to the Divine light of the perfect union of the love of God."[20] There is a way of loving in the darkness.

I wait, and I ask myself whether there is only a lifelong rotation— whether the darkness and the light, the blindness and the seeing, the hiding and the disclosing, the losing and the finding (as in many of Jesus' parables) only go on and on. Does life only go 'round? Or may it be that what is found is more than what was lost because of the finding, that what is seen is now more clearly seen because of the darkness, that what is loved is now more dearly treasured because it was lost? Do I merely want to believe or do I experience the possibility of a gyre?—spiraling from its initial plane—rising above the horizon to where all life can be seen, where we may glimpse that

> Darkness is not dark to you;
> the night is as bright as the day;
> darkness and light to you are both alike.
> (Ps. 139:12)

9 | PAUL'S STORY

And to keep me from being too elated by the abundance of revelations, a thorn was given me in the flesh, a messenger of Satan, to harass me, to keep me from being too elated. Three times I prayed to the Lord to rid me of it, but he answered, "My grace is all you need; power comes to full strength in weakness." I will all the more gladly boast of my weaknesses, that the power of Christ will come and rest upon me. That is why I am quite content, for Christ's sake, with weakness, contempt, persecution, hardship, and frustration; for when I am weak, then am I strong.

2 Cor. 12:7–10

Although at times trying to disguise his feelings, Paul was a deeply wounded man when he wrote these words. They are part of a letter in which the apostle uses both irony and sarcasm to chide his recent Corinthian converts. They have been so quick to follow different teachings about their new faith and then to pride themselves on superior enlightenment and spiritual gifts. Their boasting and their fickleness were deeply disturbing and a source of personal anguish to Paul. To add to his consternation some of the Corinthians were evidently also poking fun at him, making jokes about him and his concerns. Nor did they appreciate or like the fact that Paul had not requested support while he was among them. The Corinthians preferred leaders who asked for monetary offerings. Likely they also valued the subtle strings of obligation that resulted from their acceptance.

Partly because of their emotional depths it is difficult to be precise about the issues that lay at the bottom of this rift. It may also be, in the way of human affairs, that Paul himself had difficulty in determining the character of the problems. The wellsprings of human emotions and actions are always difficult to plumb and, no doubt, there were many different motivations among the Corinthians. Added to this, Paul was writing from Ephesus, over two hundred difficult sea miles distant from Corinth. All his information was reaching him second or third hand.

111

Moreover, since there is no record of there having been any direct response from the Corinthians themselves, we are left with only Paul's interpretation of the circumstances and our own efforts at reading between the lines as we attempt to reconstruct the attitudes of the Corinthians.[1]

Yet the broad outlines of the situation do emerge from under the impress of Paul's passionate reply to what he has heard. Certain of the Corinthians have decided that Paul's presentation of the Christian faith and his leadership are not sufficient for them. They have shown themselves ready—even eager—to accept different or at least additional teachings about Jesus and the activity of the Holy Spirit. They claim to have attained to a yet better way, a higher religious knowledge. They have given their attention to representatives of other Christian communities who, they believe, present the gospel more eloquently and powerfully. Archly but also angrily Paul refers to these individuals who have so swayed his flock as "these superlative apostles" (2 Cor. 11:5 and 12:11).

Efforts have been made to trace more definitively the teachings of these superlative apostles. Some have thought them to have come from Jerusalem and to be insisting that the Corinthians adhere more closely to Jewish tenets and practices. Others have seen them as "gnostics," setting forth a secret and extra-worldly *wisdom* as necessary for salvation. Their followers would be granted special visions and revelations that would set them apart from ordinary believers. They could regard themselves as already *risen* to a spiritual plane of life. Very likely these apostles presented themselves as men able to work wonders and miracles.[2]

It is quite possible that various religious strains were mixed together in their version of the gospel. Corinth was a city of many religions. A seaport and trading center that had been refounded and rebuilt only a century earlier, it was populated by people who came from different countries and cultures. This gave to the locale a rather exotic syncretistic flavor along with a reputation for instability and licentiousness. We know that Paul had to deal with some sticky problems among his recalcitrant recruits, ranging from their indifference to the significance of an incestuous relationship to the misuse of spiritual gifts. In this spicy seaport, open to the flow of new ideas and practices, it would hardly be surprising if certain Jewish teachings were mixed with other religious beliefs and observances and used as evidence of a superior religious knowledge and power.

However imprecise Paul's knowledge of the Corinthians' beliefs and of their ideas about signs of special eminence, the spiritual dangers were clear. The Corinthians were in fact acting in a quite "worldly fashion,"[3] making use of criteria that were the opposite of genuine faith. They were interpreting power and spiritual strength by the world's standards, not those of the crucified Christ. Paul realized, however, that his counter-attack had to be a complex maneuver. He needed to wage a coordinated campaign on several fronts. First, insisting always that he was being forced to do so and that he was speaking "as a fool," Paul himself could "boast of worldly things" (2 Cor. 11:18)—of revelations and visions. Second, he could certainly claim an excellent Jewish lineage. And further, if they wanted to talk about who was a true servant of Christ, Paul was able to present a catalogue of hardships and dangers he would more than match against anyone else's list. He was a fool, of course, to boast in this manner for no one should be commending himself before God. The true power came from God and his strength could never be described in such worldly terms.

The argument wells up from a man who is at once angry and injured, and who needs both to contradict and to reconcile. Although at times painfully obvious, the appeal is still subtle in its effects. *You want to boast, do you? I can go you far better. Yet, in our boasting how easily we could all become deaf to the heartbeat of what it means to be a Christian.* "I am not," Paul insists, "in the least inferior to these superlative apostles, even though I am nothing" (2 Cor. 12:11).

It is in this context that Paul refers to his personal problem, his thorn in the flesh. It is for him a touchy issue indeed. Evidently some of the Corinthians had been critical of Paul himself and not just his ideas. We find here one of the early rounds of a game that Christians would often play: "We are spiritually stronger than you," or today it might be called "The Charisma Game." Not only does our side have more and better revelations and visions, but the words and presence of our new leaders convey more spiritual authority. Earlier in this letter, Paul, stung by rumors, parenthetically and sarcastically alludes to what he has heard them saying about him: "I who am humble when face to face with you, but bold when I am away." A little later he is more explicit. He has heard that it was said of him, "His letters are weighty and strong, but his bodily presence is weak and his speech is of no account." A moment afterward he rubs the wound again, "Even if I am unskilled in speaking . . ." (2 Cor. 10:1, 10, 11; 11:6).

In an earlier letter Paul had told the Corinthians that he never intended to come before them as though he were a great orator.

> For I decided to know nothing among you except Jesus Christ and him crucified. And I was with you in weakness and in much fear and trembling; and my speech and my message were not in plausible words of wisdom, but in demonstrations of Spirit and power.
>
> (1 Cor. 1:2–4)

Paul then reminds his wayward disciples that, when he was among them, there were signs—mighty works—that were demonstrations of his apostolic authority (2 Cor. 12:12). On the one hand, he seems to want to respond to this effect: *You'll see who presents the gospel with boldness when necessary—you who like it when these other disciples lord it over you.* Yet from both personal experience and theological reflection Paul recognizes this cannot be the whole answer, and he asks the Corinthians to ponder with him a mystery of Christian living.

This thorn, Paul says, was given him in the flesh. Although he pleaded three times in earnest prayer that it should be taken from him, he had to learn to live with it. Some readers have guessed that Paul is alluding not to a particular ailment but to a more general condition of this life that he had to endure. From his sometimes rather feisty manner and his sensitivity to remarks about his physical presence it has, for instance, been inferred that he might have been a rather short man. Obviously he could do nothing about his stature, and it is unlikely he expected the Lord to do anything about it either, but it could be surmised that he needed help through prayer in dealing with his own attitude toward his appearance.

On the whole, however, it seems improbable that Paul is speaking figuratively with reference to an essentially emotional or spiritual ailment. While it is true that the apostle sometimes uses the word *flesh* to include the whole realm of human experience that does not show faith toward God, the context here suggests a specific physical problem. There are indications too that it may have interfered with Paul's missionary work. It could have been among the reasons why he had to postpone at least one previous trip he had planned to make to Corinth (for which postponement he was also criticized) and be related to the condition that Paul mentions when writing to the Galatians. At one time, we are told, his plans for travel had been so disrupted that he had to make an unscheduled stop in the communities of Galatia.

> You know that it was because of a bodily aliment that I originally preached the gospel to you; and though my condition was a trial to you, you did not scorn or despise me, but received me as an angel of God, as Jesus Christ. (Gal. 4:13–14)

Here we may also find another clue for our long-range medical diagnosis of what Paul describes as a thorn in his flesh. If the same ailment troubled Paul both in Galatia and during the period of his correspondence with the Corinthians, it may have been of a kind to cause him to worry about possible contemptuous treatment—about which Paul was certainly highly sensitive.

As our final clue, we should probably take seriously that which Paul describes as the harrassing character of his problem. In addition to being on occasion disabling, it was also an irritant. Perhaps it was one of those conditions that seem to become better, only suddenly to worsen at the most inopportune times.

There has been no lack of suggestions. Everything from hemorrhoids, to facial neuralgia, to epilepsy has been put forward to explain Paul's lament.[4] A condition causing stammering has also been inferred and might help explain why Paul felt his problem to be a trial to the Galatians and a potential cause of scorn, and why also certain Corinthians may have belittled him for being a poor speaker. What a painful irony that would be: the one sent to speak the word of the risen Christ has difficulty getting his words out!

The diagnosis of an eye condition has a few pieces of evidence for support. Immediately after mentioning his ailment to the Galatians, Paul continued: "Had it been possible you would have plucked out your eyes and given them to me" (Gal. 4:15). No doubt here the thought may be figuratively expressed, but, together with other clues, it has led some interpreters to suggest that poor eyesight or even spells of near blindness were Paul's difficulty. They point out the strong probability that Paul dictated rather than wrote at least most of his correspondence. Near the end of the letter to the Galatians he adds a kind of postscript: "See with what large letters I am now writing to you in my own hand" (Gal. 6:11).[5] One pictures a squinting figure, perhaps also wracked by headaches, bent over the writing table scrawling a few last personal concerns.

A final hint may be picked up from the story of Paul's calling to be an apostle as presented in three differing retellings in the Acts of the Apostles (9:1–19; 22:6–16; 26:12–18).[6] This experience was so intense that it caused a period of temporary blindness, reversed only by the laying on of hands and Paul's awareness of the presence of the Holy Spirit. In whatever manner this vivid religious experience is understood, it has been suggested that it bore some relationship to the physical problem by which Paul continued to be troubled.[7] Again there is irony: the very experience of his calling leaves him in a weakened condition to carry out his mission. Enlightened by his new vision of God, he has trouble seeing well enough to exercise his ministry.

In the immediate context of his imploring debate with the Corinthians, Paul is not concerned to describe or dwell upon his condition of weakness. Rather does he set forth the paradox that his illness is an illustration of one of God's ways of being present to his creation. "Power," the Lord responds to Paul's entreaty for a cure, "is made perfect in weakness" (2 Cor. 12:9).

Paul cannot afford in the course of this argument fully to explore the theology of how this should be so, but he supplies aspects of it in other portions of his correspondence with the Corinthians. Such weaknesses and frailties are, first of all, reminders that it is God's initiative and not human strength or virtue that makes salvation possible. "God chose what is low and despised in this world—mere nothings—in order to overthrow existing values. There is no place for human pride in the presence of God" (1 Cor. 1:28). "We have this treasure in earthen vessels to show that the transcendent power does not come from us but is God's alone" (2 Cor. 4:7). This truth is demonstrated over and again in Paul's ministry.

> We are afflicted in every way, but never crushed; perplexed, but never driven to despair; we have been persecuted, but never deserted; struck down, but never destroyed. (2 Cor. 4:8–9)

In the context of human fragility, God's purpose can and will continue. Christian apostles do not always, by any means, appear to come out evident winners. But "My grace is all you need" (2 Cor. 12:9). The Lord tells Paul to carry on despite his personal difficulty.

Yet God, Paul believes, does not just burden his followers with this difficult way of disclosing the true nature of his power. At the heart of the Christian experience there is a still more profound mystery. Not only in the life and resurrection of the man Jesus but also in his passion and death God himself has been revealed. The cross is his signature,[8] expressing in human history that which is always true of God's character—his willingness to share in the heartbreak and agony of life, to accept them as part of his own existence, while seeking to bring to them a new meaning.[9]

To many in his audience, Paul recognizes, this will seem passing strange. From the Jewish perspective God's presence in the world was expected to be accompanied by unmistakable signs of divine might. Those more inclined to a Greek way of viewing life looked for a God who would speak authoritatively to the human desire to understand and to have a rational comprehension of the purposes of creation. But Paul is charged with presenting an unexpected kind of savior—certainly no religious hero by the world's standards.[10] "Jews call for miracles, Greeks look for wisdom; instead we proclaim Christ crucified, a stumbling block to Jews and folly to the Gentiles" (1 Cor. 1:22–23).[11] Only those who have come to genuine faith, Paul contends, will begin to catch sight of the paradox that it is through such lowliness that the true power and wisdom of God are revealed.

Difficult as this insight is to grasp and maintain, it obviously parallels teachings of Jesus as remembered by his disciples. We recall his unwillingness to perform miracles just to prove that God's kingdom was active in the world. This is illustrated by the story of his triumph over Satan's greatest temptation: Jesus refuses to leap from the pinnacle of the temple to land unharmed amid the awed crowd below. Other words and actions press home the awareness that his way begins in humility and not with power and exaltation as the world would understand them. Those who would enter the kingdom must do so as children (Mark 10:15). "Any one who would be first, must be last of all and servant of all" (Mark 9:35; see Mark 10:43–44). Those who would be Jesus' disciples must pick up their crosses and follow him (Mark 8:34). The way of love's reconciliation leads through the valley of Gethsemane to the hill of Calvary. Even Jesus' resurrection might have become but one of the sensations of history, open to any number of understandings, were it not first interpreted by the drama of his passion. No miracle saves him from the loneliness and desolation of this death which all must face.

Paul begins to perceive why this must be so. Caring and creativity always involve the necessity of pain and suffering.[12] To form and maintain a relationship is inevitably to open oneself to compassion (the *suffering with* the other in times of hurt and darkness) and the injury that wittingly or unwittingly another will cause. Marriage, parenthood, and close friendship are our chief paradigms for these experiences.

This compassion together with its vulnerability are God's chosen ways of relating to the world. Thus in Jesus he participates in the rich color and pageantry, but also in the pain and frustration of human life. He expresses his will to rule not primarily from above but from within, not from outside but from inside the limitations of human history. By sharing so fully in the human condition the Creator and Lord of the universe establishes, through a love without any coercive force, the strongest sense of relationship with his creatures. On the surface—to apparent human knowledge—this must seem a form of weakness. Yet the bond so formed, Paul maintains, is powerful beyond human measure. "The foolishness of God is wiser than men, and the weakness of God is stronger than men" (1 Cor. 1:25).

As a disciple Paul finds that his own story has to be told in the imitation of Christ.[13] There has been no need for us in this chaper fully to redramatize Paul's story because it is already a retelling, another version of the story of Paul's Lord. Paul experiences the healing power of the gospel but he also finds suffering to be part of his vocation. He suggests to the Corinthians that in this, one may perceive the God of Jesus Christ still active in the world. Paul (or one of his followers) later touches again upon this mystery. "It is now my joy to suffer for you. This is my way of helping to complete, in my poor human flesh, the full tale of Christ's afflictions still to be endured" (Col. 1:24). God, in Christ, is in the world loving and suffering in his disciple. The tale continues on—not yet complete, still requiring suffering, while moving toward a fulfillment that will consummate God's purposes for creation. "The Bible directs man to God's powerlessness and suffering," wrote Dietrich Bonhoeffer. "It is not the religious act that makes the Christian, but participation in the sufferings of God in the secular life. It is allowing oneself to be caught up in the messianic suffering of God in Jesus Christ."[14]

All who would be disciples, Paul realizes, must expect that their stories will be part of this story. It is not that they are deliberately to seek suffering. Such a negative pursuit would be a virtual parody of love's concern for the self as well as others. What they seek is caring and relationship which necessitates compassion. Following Christ, their vocation is to find companionship with others, especially with those who are in need of healing—the sick, the outcast, and the oppressed. In love they are to share with them. The suffering is not asked for but is accepted when it comes. So Jesus on the night before he died prayed, "Abba, Father, everything is possible for you. Take this cup away from me. But let it be as you, not I, would have it" (Mark 14:36).

Some of the suffering experienced will be the physical and mental pain that would come to any human being, no matter what his or her vocation. At times we are probably too glib in thinking that our difficulties are the result of Christian discipleship when they are but part of the lot of every human life. Affliction may, however, as in Paul's case, be made harder to bear by the work of discipleship. And all suffering can by an act of the will be offered up and associated with the suffering of God as chiefly expressed in Jesus. A most notable example of this joining of suffering with Christ's on behalf of others was Pope John XXIII's prayers for and with others during his final illness.

But certainly some of the suffering of discipleship—in ministry to the sick and dying, in sharing in some way in the circumstances and even the persecution of the disliked and the oppressed—will be affliction that one might have avoided. It is painful to watch a patient one loves die. It can be difficult to live without what others have, or to be ridiculed for associating with the not-so-respectable or fashionable. Such suffering, however, builds powerful bonds of solidarity to help in the comforting and healing of individual lives and of broken relationships in society.[15]

The repeated message of Christian experience is that those who are close to God suffer with him. Often today one meets people who speak of their desire to be closer to God—even to have visions of the divine life. Many of them perhaps will. But they must also learn that to share with God means to share his vision of human beings as he has done in Jesus; and to care for, accept, and forgive others means to suffer with them.

We understand now, however, why Paul can also call that suffering a joy,[16] for in and through the suffering love is found, and the way to the redemption—the revaluing—of all things is discovered. With Paul, following in the imitation of Christ, others can learn not only to accept the hardships and pain but to affirm their purpose. In so doing one begins to be able to affirm the value of the entire creative process while yet recognizing the cost. With God one says *yes* to life as opposed to not-life, to existence with its suffering in contrast to the absence of suffering were creation not to have been risked. This Creator God is the true and great God—the God worth believing and trusting in. It is he who proclaims through his prophet, "I make the light, I create the darkness; I make good fortune and create woe. I, the Lord, do all these things" (Isa. 45:7). This is the only God who can revalue all the world's suffering and evil. He redeems not by escaping from the painful aspects of creative activity, but by entering in and accepting these consequences. "I have made, and I will bear; I will carry, and I will save" (Isa. 46:4).

If these thoughts provide insight into the character of God's power and way of relationship with the world, one must expect, as Paul learned, the necessity of bearing ill-health and suffering along with the possibilities for healing. Once more Paul discovers a seeming paradox about God's power. On the one hand, through Jesus and through Paul's own ministry, God can and does work cures. "The signs of a true apostle were performed among you in all patience, with signs and wonders and mighty works" (2 Cor. 12:12).[17] On the other hand, as in Paul's own case, there is sometimes no physical healing—only the faithful endurance of affliction and further suffering. And then there is the example of God's chosen one. Alone on the cross, he was mocked: "He saved others; he cannot save himself. Let the Christ, the King of Israel, come down now from the cross, that we may see and believe" (Mark 15:31–32). Jesus calls out, "My God, my God, why have you forsaken me" (Mark 15:34). A God this weak must seem to many like no God at all—an absent God, virtually another way of presenting atheism.[18] Yet this is the God in whom Jesus and Paul continued to trust.

Paul and Jesus were part of an age that held a world view very different from our own. Mysterious, transcendent powers directly controlled many events from the daily rising of the sun, to earthquakes and plagues. Today most of us understand natural events quite differently. We are trained to look for the causes of things that happen within a closely knit relationship of causes and effects (however difficult it may be to establish a determinative link between a particular event and its cause).[19] While God may be conceived of as the original and ultimate or final cause for all natural and life events, we have trouble thinking of him as the stage manager for every happening, or even as the great intervenor who directs the course of selected events. Recall the problem we earlier posed for ourselves when discussing intercessory prayer.[20] What goes through our minds when we hear someone pray for Bill and Mary who are traveling by car today? Do we see God hovering over the traffic intersections enabling the cars to pass safely, afterwards giving him credit for Bill and Mary's safe arrival at their destination? But what then about Tom and Sue (for whom others were praying) who ended their lives in flaming and bloody wreckage just minutes after Bill and Mary had passed the same intersection? Had God gone away for the moment, or did he, for reasons unknown to us, direct the crash?

Problems such as these provide dilemmas for contemporary Christians who want to believe in a God who cares but who also want to trust in a real God in a real world—a world in which babies are born and sometimes die, where bodies glory in their strength and then grow old and diseased or are sometimes mangled in accidents. They cannot find faith in a context that requires the make-believe of thinking in a way contrary to the best efforts to understand how life and natural forces function.

Even though their world views were different from ours, Paul and Jesus, through their understanding of the role of suffering, anticipated our modern problems in comprehending God's relationship to the creation and helped to point us in the direction of understanding. Given the existence of God, one might think in simple terms of five basic ways God could relate to the world. (1) He operates everything by direct action. (2) He has created the world to be self-sustaining and self-regulating (at least over a process of billions of years), but he still intervenes frequently in its operations. (3) Same as 2, except that he intervenes only on very special occasions. (4) The world was set to go like a clock. God observes but never interferes with the design of his original workmanship. (5) The world has been created to operate on its own self-sustaining principles which God does not alter. He participates, however, in the world through his compassionate sharing in the experience of human lives.

Jesus on the cross and Paul with his recalcitrant Corinthians and thorn in the flesh found themselves in relationship with a God who did not intervene. He was visibly absent in the world; yet they found him to be invisibly present. He did not stand aloof but participated with them in their sufferings, and, in so doing, helped them to transform their meaning.

Sometimes that sharing may lead to physical healing. The power, however, whether it results in such healing or the transformation of suffering, is of the same character. It is not a divine intervention in the natural processes of the world, but God's compassion mediated through human lives—bringing about acceptance and forgiveness—sometimes healing and sometimes calling forth and supporting a witness to love through suffering.

While Paul is able to boast to the Corinthians of the healings and wonders that God's love can work, he also perceived the dangers of such a presentation of the Christian faith. How easy it was and is for true religion to be misconceived. The enemy of faith in the God of Jesus, Paul realized, is not doubt, but superstition and magic posing as religion, for this means belief in another kind of god—a god who might be controlled and directed by human religious devices.[21] People might well boast if by their superior spiritual power they could so direct God's operations.

But Paul was given this thorn in the flesh. While still struggling to find the ideas and language to frame his insight, he had begun to learn that God's greatest strength was shown not through miracles but through compassionate love. The mightiness of God revealed on the cross could also be disclosed through Paul's frailty in order that once more "power might come to full strength through weakness."

One sympathizes with Paul, probably short of stature, troubled and hampered by some annoying and perhaps embarrassing ailment. He was up against these healthy, suntanned, handsome apostles direct from the holy city Jerusalem.[22] He could not even cure his own disability, while they probably claimed to be healing people left and right. Nonetheless, in the face of the Corinthians' disparagement of his weak presence and lack of evident spiritual power, Paul will

> all the more gladly boast of my weakness, that the power of Christ may rest upon me. I am, then, well content for the sake of Christ with weakness, insults, persecution, hardship and frustration; for when I am weak, then am I strong.
>
> (2 Cor. 12:9–10)

Paul's story thus becomes a model and inspiration for all persons with handicaps. Since all of us have or will have handicaps of some kind, his story becomes a model for everyone. Those who are handicapped can become strongest.

No doubt it is easier to discover in retrospect how such a providence might be active in one's life. That is why we need to rehearse and reflect—to probe beneath the surfaces of our life's stories. Paul could point to one illustration, when he reminded the Galatians that it was because of bodily illness that he was given the opportunity to preach the good news about Jesus to them. It also seems likely that the illness forced him to spend a longer time in the area than he normally did in the towns he visited. One may imagine that in his weakened condition he had to let the Galatians provide some ministry to him and that, when he did preach the gospel, he could not do it as forcefully as he would have liked. Did this mean that the Galatians were given an inferior version of the Christian message or left unimpressed by their missionary? On the contrary. Although they at times wavered in their full acceptance of its implications, the gospel appears to have taken firm root among them, and one can believe that their bond with Paul was strengthened by the occasion of sharing with him in his distress.

Looking back, Paul could also begin to see how his emotional out-pouring to the Corinthians could have deepened their caring for him and for one another. While his heated displays of emotion (particularly in an earlier letter which made blunt criticism regarding the sexual behavior of an individual and the Corinthians' attitude toward this) might be seen as signs of weakness, which in one sense Paul regretted, this exposure of his naked self also had helped Paul to move the hearts of the Corinthians as no other power was able to do. "I wrote you out of much affection and anguish of heart and with many tears, not to cause you pain, but to let you know the abundant love I have for you" (2 Cor. 2:4).

If we correctly interpret the order of his correspondence with the new disciples in Corinth (for the two epistles now found in the Bible actually appear to have been composed from four or five letters),[23] we are fortunate to have a glimpse into the aftermath of Paul's fervent pleas. Apparently Paul, traveling the land route through Macedonia on his way to pay the promised visit to Corinth, had commissioned his friend

Titus to precede him. There may have been a logistical reason for sending this advance man, but it was also Paul's way of checking out what manner of reception he was likely to find. He was concerned not only about how his pointed remarks and sarcasms had been received, but by the criticism he had apparently generated by his failure to follow through on earlier intentions to return to Corinth.[24] This delay may in part have been occasioned by such a serious bout with his affliction that it had caused him even to despair of life and to feel that he had received "a sentence of death" (2 Cor. 1:8–9). Likely he was still in a somewhat weakened condition. Titus would at least provide some indication of the lay of the land.

And thanks be to God! Although at first all the more concerned when Titus did not meet him in Troas, Paul finally was reunited with him in Macedonia and there received the good news.

> Even when we reached Macedonia there was no relief for this poor body of ours. Instead we found trouble at every turn, quarrels all around with foreboding in our heart. But God, who comforts the downcast, comforted us by the coming of Titus, and not merely by his arrival, but because of his being so greatly comforted by you. He has told us of your longing for me, how sorry you are and how eager to take my side, so that I am happier still.
>
> Even if I did wound you by my letter, I do not now regret it. I may have been sorry for it when I saw that the letter caused you pain, even if only for a little while; but now I am happy, not that your feelings were wounded, but because the wound led to a change of heart.
>
> (2 Cor. 7:5–9)

So does Paul learn yet more of God's providence—how through his illness and the frailty of his emotions God's love can reach out to others.

> Honor and dishonor, praise and blame, all come to us. We are treated as imposters who yet speak the truth—unknown men who are yet well known. Dying we still live on; though disciplined by suffering, we are not done to death. In our sorrows, we always find cause for rejoicing. Although ourselves poor, we bring riches to many. Penniless, we yet possess everything.
>
> (2 Cor. 6:8–10)

Through the sharing of his weakness, Paul has discovered again the power of God which was most decisively revealed on a cross.

It is a lesson taught over and again to the one who would minister. We think we are effective only when we are powerful—in charge. We can help only when we have all the words, the prayers, the resources. But then one day we do not. We are tired, overwhelmed, perhaps irritable. Our own faith may be frail, our behavior not exemplary. All the weakness of our humanity is apparent. And on that day we discover that a person we have never been able to touch before can suddenly join hands with us.[25]

One thinks again of Pope John slowly dying and dedicating his suffering and the ebbing of life to all others living in pain and fear. Did ever a papal bull or the high, solemn panoply of Vatican liturgy—or, for that matter, even a reported miracle—reach out with such power to minister?

The power of the love which comes to full strength in weakness is different from all other power we experience. Its exercise does not result in the control of others; it effects their empowerment. The fact that one has more need not mean another has less. Indeed, the more that power is shared, the more power there is. Our intermittent perceptions of this truth are perhaps our glimpses into the divine love which Paul says "will never come to an end." "There is nothing love cannot face; there is no limit to its faith, its hope, its endurance" (1 Cor. 13:7–8). It will continue when all other powers have dimmed and faded.

Yet these are lessons hard to learn, at times hard even to remember. For myself I find that time and again I must go and ask once more if this is what God means, that his followers—those who are trying to do his ministry—should have to endure such weakness and hardships. It has taken me a long time to come to the point of actually saying how I feel. There is so much in the practice of religion which suggests that we ought not let God know if we are frustrated and angry. But the more I read some of the psalms and the laments of the prophets and hear the catharsis of the outpouring of their pain, the less inhibited I become.

Paul knew these same cries from the heart, and we can imagine him kneeling in his dark room in Ephesus:

Why have you cast me off, Lord? Why have you hidden your face from me? There is so much suffering, Lord. Here I am, imperfect as I am, trying to help. You called me to this ministry. I have tried to obey—going where your Spirit seemed to lead. But I can't do it without physical stamina. Again I beg of you: remove this thorn in my flesh. Give me my full strength and power back again. Let me show these Corinthians. Let me do your work.

And then the response: "My grace is all you need; power comes to full strength in weakness."

Some of Paul's shortcomings remain very evident to us. Often one meets a Christian who remarks (with perhaps a trace of smugness), "I don't really much care for Paul. He does, after all, complain quite a lot and, one way or another, get in his full share of boasting." One has to guess that there were some who knew him in person who would have held him in less than high esteem—John Mark,[26] for example, and probably Peter,[27] certainly some of the Corinthians. Archly they would have agreed with Paul's contention that "we have this treasure in earthen vessels" (2 Cor. 4:7). Nevertheless, it was part of Paul's greatness as a Christian to recognize his true strength, even though he had continually to rediscover it.

Had Paul the opportunity to collect and edit his correspondence in the manner of a modern-day person of reknown, he would certainly have been tempted to tone down many of his remarks to the Corinthians. In dispassionate hindsight he might not have wanted others to see how much he was hurting and how his pain had provoked him to a heavy-handed sarcasm and personal pleading that might be regarded as manipulative. But we can be grateful that this opportunity was never given to Paul. In his letters genuine humanity is graphic—with all its triumphs and passions, its rejoicing and humbling. The theology of the apostle lives in the authenticity of his story.

It is as he told the Corinthians: the power is not in his eloquence. The majesty is not to be perceived in the miracles, revelations, or visions. Yes, Paul says, I have these too, but they are not at the heart of faith. At the heart of faith is the trust and the faithfulness by which the disciple, whom God in his graciousness has accepted, lives. This is the beginning of the true miracle—that men and women find the power, in the midst of mortal frailties and frustrations, to carry on in caring for one another and in trying to present the gospel of the crucified God. The miracle deepens as through the sharing of weakness and suffering a greater sense of human caring and knowing of one another is realized. And as shared poverty brings enrichment—as power comes to strength in weakness—passion reaches toward resurrection.

We have in our records but a few chapters in the story of Paul's relationship with his Corinthian disciples. We do not know the end of the tale. Probably, in the way of most human stories, there was no truly final denouement. Life with its complex strands of interwoven narratives went on. Clement of Rome, writing a generation or two later, tells us that the Corinthians continued to be a fractious and contentious bunch.[28] It would not surprise us if Paul was wounded yet once more. Maybe, when he actually arrived in Corinth for his long-promised visit, there were further complaints, new problems, more questioning of his authority and *power,* much as he had feared.[29] (2 Cor. 12:20–21). One can imagine Paul returning to his lodgings, sick at heart again. Maybe his thorn in the flesh nagged unmercifully. He knew once more something of the pain and abandonment of his Lord. He knelt and felt himself with those first onlookers wondering still again about the kind of God who would not come down from the cross but who will not leave him alone.

NOTES

INTRODUCTION

1. Earlier in this century the Gospel of Mark was still regarded by many as an authentic chronological outline of Jesus' ministry. It came to be seen, however, that the evangelist had little definitive knowledge of the general sequence of events in Jesus' ministry and that the temporal links between stories were often quite vague and marked by the author's editorial style. The individual stories were like beads on a string, the string being Mark's narrative connection of the stories. But since the string itself did not reach back to Jesus' ministry, it could be cut by those who wished to probe behind the Gospel. One now had a handful of beads, each of which could be examined on its own to see how it might have been passed along in the tradition before coming to the evangelist. With reference to the pioneering work of Rudolf Bultmann and Martin Dibelius in the development of this exploration of the traditions or, as it came to be called, form-criticism, see E. V. McKnight, *What Is Form Criticism?* (Philadelphia: Fortress Press, 1969). More particularly, see "The Form-Critical Approach: Miracles in the World of the New Testament" in *Miracles in Dispute: A Continuing Debate,* by Ernst and Mary-Luise Keller (Philadelphia: Fortress Press, 1969), pp. 120–30. On the *form* of healing stories see p. 40 in our discussion of Legion.

2. It has long been thought that the fourth evangelist made use of a collection of epiphanies or "signs" of Jesus. Such a collection would have been a kind of miniature Gospel with its own theological perspective. See D. M. Smith, *The Composition and Order of the Fourth Gospel* (New Haven: Yale University Press, 1956) and R. T. Fortna, *The Gospel of Signs* (New York: Cambridge University Press, 1970). On the possibility that cycles of stories were used by Mark in his Gospel, see P. T. Achtemeier, "Toward the Isolation of Pre-Markan Miracle Catenae," *JBL* 89 (1970): 265–91; and "The Origin and Function of the Pre-Markan Miracle Catenae," *JBL* 91 (1972): 198–221.

3. Only a few decades ago the evangelists were seen mostly as collectors who fitted together an already fixed body of materials. It is now widely recognized that the evangelists were themselves creative authors and theologians—shaping and adding, using context, juxtaposition, and composition to deal with the questions and concerns of their own times. See Norman Perrin, *What Is Redaction Criticism?* (Philadelphia: Fortress Press, 1969).

4. A helpful overview of the history of the understanding of biblical miracles and the changing attitudes toward them is provided by Keller and Keller in *Miracles in Dispute.*

5. It may be that "blessed is he who takes no offense at me" was a way of

saying, "Do not let these acts become a cause of difficulty, as though I am only seeking to draw attention to myself; they point to the new age." One must also observe, however, that from the perspective of the developing tradition the passage has obvious apologetic purposes. It especially helps to enlighten the true character of Jesus' mission, showing that his miracles were not mere wonders (such as other great figures of the time might have performed) but messianic deeds indicating that he was the promised "coming one." See Anton Fridrichsen, *The Problem of Miracle in Primitive Christianity*, trans. Roy A. Harrisville and John S. Hanson (Minneapolis: Augsburg Publishing House, 1972), pp. 95–102.

6. Isa. 29:18–19; 35:5–6; 61:1.

7. Norman Perrin, *Jesus and the Language of the Kingdom* (Philadelphia: Fortress Press, 1976), p. 42. Similarly, cf. Perrin's *The New Testament: An Introduction* (New York: Harcourt Brace Jovanovich, 1974), p. 284. For a present-day Jewish perspective that strongly emphasizes a view of Jesus as a charismatic healer, see Geza Vermes, *Jesus the Jew* (Philadelphia: Fortress Press, 1981).

8. Hans Küng, *On Being A Christian* (New York: Doubleday & Co., 1976), p. 229. A useful statement regarding the centrality of the healing ministry to the Gospels and to Jesus is by Pierson Parker, "Early Christianity as a Religion of Healing," *The Saint Luke's Journal of Theology* 19 (1976): 142–50.

9. For other Gospel accusations that Jesus was in league with Satan, see Mark 3:22 and Matt. 9:34; John 7:20; 8:48–52; 10:2. Cf. also Matt. 10:25. Matt. 9:32–34 is of particular interest in that the accusation ("He casts out demons by the prince of demons") comes just after Jesus has healed a dumb demoniac. It is a clear parallel to Luke 11:14–23; Matt. 12:22–30. The parallel may be Matthew's creation, but it suggests the possibility of an older tradition.

With respect to the tradition of hostility toward Jesus' miracles on the part of both Jews and pagans (with the frequent charge that he was a charlatan) see Fridrichsen, *The Problem of Miracle in Primitive Christianity*, pp. 85–118. In the Babylonian Talmud, tractate Sanhedrin 43a, for example, it is said that Jeshua (i.e., Jesus) was hanged because he practiced sorcery.

10. See D. E. Nineham, *The Use and Abuse of the Bible: A Study of the Bible in an Age of Rapid Cultural Change* (New York: Harper and Row, 1976).

11. E. C. Hobbs dramatically emphasizes this difference by comparing the genre of miracle stories in the New Testament, not with contemporary stories of religious healing, but with television commercials, wherein various ills are instantly cured by the touted products. "Gospel Miracle Story and Modern Miracle Stories," *ATR*, supplementary ser. 3, ed. M. H. Shepherd, Jr., and E. C. Hobbs (March 1974), pp. 117–26.

12. See my discussion and proposals in "Ears That Hear and Do Not Hear: Fundamental Hearing of the Bible," in *Scripture Today*, ed. Durstan R. McDonald (Wilton, Conn.: Morehouse-Barlow, 1980), pp. 23–49. On the importance for the appropriation of the Bible of a dialogue between present-day experience and that of the Bible, see Edward Schillebeeckx, *Christ: The Experience of Jesus as Lord* (New York: Seabury Press, 1980), pp. 29–79.

13. See Stephen Crites, "The Narrative Quality of Experience," *JAAR* 39 (1971): 291–311; Brian Wicker, *The Story-Shaped World: Fiction and Metaphysics: Some Variations on a Theme* (Notre Dame, Ind.: University of Notre Dame Press, 1975); and J. D. Crossan, *The Dark Interval: Towards a Theology of Story* (Niles, Ill.: Argus Communications, 1975). "Art," maintains John Dixon, "is not an ornament to an existing world, it is the primary means of forming the world." *Art and the Theological Imagination* (New York: Seabury Press, 1978), p. 12.

14. Sallie McFague, *Speaking in Parables: A Study in Metaphor and Theology* (Philadelphia: Fortress Press, 1975), p. 138.

15. On the function of narrative reticence in the Jewish scriptures, see Robert Alter, *The Art of Biblical Narrative* (New York: Basic Books, 1981), esp. chap. 6.

16. See Walter Wink, *Transforming Bible Study: A Leader's Guide* (Nashville: Abingdon Press, 1980). Several of my purposes are similar to his.

17. A. C. Thiselton, "The New Hermeneutic," in *New Testament Interpretation: Essays on Principles and Methods,* ed. I. H. Marshall (Exeter, U.K.: Paternoster Press, 1977), p. 309.

18. See Hans Frei, *The Eclipse of Biblical Narrative: A Study in Eighteenth and Nineteenth Century Hermeneutics* (New Haven: Yale University Press, 1974).

19. Stanley Hauerwas, "Story and Theology," in *Truthfulness and Tragedy: Further Investigations into Christian Ethics* (Notre Dame, Ind.: University of Notre Dame Press, 1977), p. 77.

20. Keller and Keller, *Miracles in Dispute,* p. 246.

21. For additional material on the understanding of the demonic, see especially chap. 4 and the chapter "Acts of Power" in *God's Parable,* F. H. Borsch (Philadelphia: Westminster Press, 1975).

22. In an important sense Matthew and Luke should be regarded as the first interpreters of Mark. The process of interpretation by transmission took on a different character once there were written Gospels, but it never stopped. See "The Transmission of the Gospel in the First Centuries," André Benoît, in *The Gospel as History,* ed. Vilmus Vajta (Philadelphia: Fortress Press, 1975), pp. 145–68. "Transmission cannot be understood as a simple repetition, a pure retelling of a message from the past. To transmit means, in a certain sense, to interpret" (p. 151).

23. See G. W. H. Lampe, "Miracles and Early Christian Apologetic," and M. F. Wiles, "Miracles in the Early Church," in *Miracles: Cambridge Studies in Their Philosophy and History,* ed. C. F. D. Moule (London: A. R. Mowbray and Co., 1965), pp. 203–18, 219–34.

CHAPTER 1

1. Inability to speak often accompanies deafness. In the story of the boy with the dumb spirit (Mark 9:14–29), Jesus rebukes "the unclean spirit, saying to it, 'You dumb and deaf spirit, I command you, come out of him.'" In the

interesting narrative, Mark 7:31–37, a man who is deaf and has an impediment in his speech is brought to Jesus. The man is healed when Jesus puts his fingers into his ears, spits and touches his tongue, and says, "Ephphatha," meaning "Be opened." This manner of symbolic, almost mimetic, healing activity is unusual in the Gospels but fairly common with other healers of the era. Note, at the end of the passage, v. 37: "He has done all things well; he even makes the deaf hear and the dumb speak." In the Matthean parallel (Matt. 12:22) to our story (Luke 11:14) the demoniac is both dumb and blind.

2. Although no act of touching is recorded in the brief Gospel narrative of the dumb man's healing (and is even less frequent in narratives explicitly involving exorcisms), it is often a feature in healing stories. See Geza Vermes, *Jesus the Jew* (Philadelphia: Fortress Press, 1981), p. 24. In Mark, see 1:31, 41; 3:10; 5:23, 28–30, 41; 6:5, 13, 56; 7:33; 8:23–25; 9:27. D. E. Nineham comments, "The gesture [of the laying on of hands] so frequently accompanied the act of healing that it came to be used as a metaphor for it." *The Gospel of St. Mark,* Pelican Gospel Commentaries (Baltimore: Penguin Books, 1963), p. 203.

CHAPTER·2

1. The *crowd* appears in the Gospels as an anonymous group, sometimes eager to see Jesus, sometimes puzzled by him, but generally either favorable or neutral. On several occasions Jesus is said to feel the need to withdraw from the press of the crowd and their desires: "It thus seems that those who merely seek marvels or are simply curious are held at a distance." R. Meyer in *Theological Dictionary of the New Testament (TDNT),* ed. G. Kittel and G. Friedrich, trans. G. W. Bromiley, 9 vols. (Grand Rapids, Mich.: Wm. B. Eerdmans, 1964–72), 5:586. Along with Jesus' warnings about right and wrong understanding of the kingdom's acts of power, the suggestion that Jesus was at least ambivalent toward the popular, crowd-attracting aspect of his ministry could reach back to authentic reminiscence.

2. Cf. Matt. 4:1–11. Matthew places the temptation to leap from the temple second, and Luke places it in the third and final position.

3. *The Brothers Karamazov* (New York: Random House, Modern Library, n.d.), p. 265.

4. On the Old Testament sense of "adulterous" as false worship, see Jer. 3:6–10.

5. On the symbolic character of Jesus' acts, see M. E. Glasswell, "The Use of Miracles in the Markan Gospel," in *Miracles: Cambridge Studies in Their Philosophy and History,* ed. C. F. D. Moule (London: A. R. Mowbray and Co., 1965), pp. 151–62. "The healings are not themselves objects of faith but pointers to faith," p. 154. See also Reginald Fuller, *Interpreting the Miracles* (Philadelphia: Westminster Press, 1963), pp. 11–15. On the Greek words used to describe miracles, see Moule, "The Vocabulary of Miracle," in *Miracles,* pp. 235–38, and Harold Remus, "Does Terminology Distinguish Early Christian from Pagan Miracles?" *JBL,* 101/4 (1982), 531–51.

6. Many houses of the time in Palestine were built with outside stairs leading to a flat roof. The roof would have been composed of wooden beams covered with straw matting, branches, and beaten-down earth. (Cf. Luke 5:19, where in his retelling of the story the roof becomes one of tile as in Greco-Roman houses.) It would not have been difficult to make a large hole in such a roof. See V. Taylor, *The Gospel According to Mark* (London: Macmillan and Co., 1951), p. 194.

7. On the dangers and benefits of the encounter with the unconscious and how it may both wound and heal, see J. A. Sanford, *Healing and Wholeness* (New York: Paulist Press, 1977). Further see U. T. Holmes, *Ministry and Imagination* (New York: Seabury Press, 1976), pp. 137–64.

8. Some sense of the relationship between states of mind and physical well-being is manifest in every culture. Mental or emotional disharmony is intimately connected with lack of physical health and stamina. In many societies, including that of ancient Israel, sickness is often viewed as the result of disharmony between the individual and God—as the result of some manner of sin. (Such *sin* need not always have been the result of a deliberate act. Any action giving offense to the divine could be sufficient.) The restoration of harmony and healing required that the sin be sacrificially propitiated, wiped away, or otherwise overcome. Any simple understanding of sickness as a punishment for sin began, however, to be questioned. This is one aspect of the Book of Job. Nowhere in the New Testament is the connection between sickness and sin made explicit. The theme does play an important role in the story of the healing of the blind man (John 9:1–41), although there it seems to be questioned by Jesus. On this issue generally see M. T. Kelsey, *Healing and Christianity: In Ancient Thought and Modern Times* (New York: Harper and Row, 1973); and D. L. Gelpi, *Pentecostal Piety* (New York: Paulist Press, 1972), pp. 7–20. We can probably best conclude that early Christianity believed that there was often a relationship between sin and sickness without insisting that all sin resulted in physical illness or that all sickness (much less injury) was the result of sin.

It is interesting to note the degree to which the idea that there is a connection between illness and individual psychic conditions has reasserted itself in contemporary circles that would not regard themselves as formally religious. Such an idea is also susceptible to the same dangers as the older religious view. Heart attacks are believed to be the result of anxiety, various cancers of depression, arthritis of suppressed anger, and so forth. Those who are diagnosed as having ulcers can be made to feel that the illness is their fault—the result of worry and feelings of insecurity. Those who would help others to gain both psychological and spiritual insights into their illnesses must also assist them to realize that no one can have full control over all the factors that come together to cause illness and that, therefore, while spiritual and mental states and physical health are frequently interrelated, no individual can assume total responsibility for ill health.

On the interrelationship from a contemporary psychological and spiritual point of view, and particularly on the idea of *harmony,* see Sanford, *Healing and Wholeness.* Also and with respect to the healing ministry of Christianity more generally, see the popular works of Francis McNutt, *Healing* and *The Power to Heal* (Notre Dame, Ind.: Ave Maria Press, 1974 and 1977). With greater reference to the ministry of medicine, see Michael Wilson, *The Church Is Healing* (London: SCM Press, 1966).

9. Thomas Merton, *Contemplative Prayer* (Garden City, N.Y.: Doubleday, Image Books, 1971), p. 107.

10. See the discussion by Karl Menninger, *Whatever Became of Sin?* (New York: Hawthorn Books, 1973).

11. It is interesting to compare word order: Mark (2:10) wrote, "authority has the Son of man to forgive sins on earth"; Matthew (9:6) wrote, "authority has the Son of man on earth to forgive sins"; and Luke (5:24) wrote "the Son of man authority has on earth to forgive sins." The words "on earth" would have had a special significance for churches wishing to strengthen their understanding that forgiveness could be proclaimed and experienced now in the name of Jesus. H. E. Tödt, *The Son of Man in the Synoptic Tradition* (Philadelphia: Westminster Press, 1965), pp. 126–30, interprets similarly the authority attributed to Jesus as Son of man in Mark 2:28; see pp. 130–33. One should also compare John 5:27 where Jesus is said to have authority to execute judgment "because he is the Son of man." As the Son of man, Jesus is understood to be able to act as the divine judge; this activity, however, does not just await the final judgment but begins now in anticipation.

12. On the difficult question of the interpretation of the Son of man designation in the Gospels, see the survey by F. H. Borsch, *The Son of Man in Myth and History* (Philadelphia: Westminster Press, 1967), chap. 1. On its place in the development of the understanding of Jesus in the early Christian communities, see R. H. Fuller, *The Foundations of New Testament Christology* (New York: Charles Scribner's Sons, 1965).

13. Matthew's interpretive statement in 9:8 may reflect an earlier play on words in the Aramaic language: the authority of the Son of man is now shared by the sons of men.

14. The classic view that a healing narrative and an originally separate controversy about the forgiveness of sins have been combined is put forward by Rudolf Bultmann, *The History of Synoptic Tradition,* trans. John Marsh (New York: Harper and Row, 1963), pp. 15–16. Usually the healing story with its introduction and conclusion is seen as comprising vv. 1–5a and 10b–12 and the controversy vv. 5b–10a, but there are slightly differing theories in this regard. See I. Maisch, *Die Heilung des Gelähmten,* Stuttgarter Bibelstudien 22 (Stuttgart: KBW, 1971): 39–48. On Mark's interpolation technique (the sandwiching of one story within another) generally, see H. C. Kee, *Community of the New Age: Studies in Mark's Gospel* (Philadelphia: Westminster Press, 1977), pp. 54ff. J. R. Donahue views the technique as having been used to highlight materials and ideas Mark wished to emphasize. See *Are You the Christ? The Trial Narrative in the Gospel of Mark,* SBLDS 10 (Missoula, Mont.: Society of Biblical Literature, 1973), pp. 81–82.

Modern scholarship perceives a general tendency in the Gospels to remake healing and miracle narratives into controversy stories. Mark 2:1–12 is part of a cycle of five stories that were probably already linked before they came into Mark's hands. In all of them the dimension of controversy seems to have been heightened. See J. Dewey, *Markan Public Debate: Literary Technique, Concentric Structure, and Theology in Mark 2:1—3:6*, SBLDS 48 (Chico, Calif.: Scholars Press, 1980). Some scholars, however, recognizing that Jesus was remembered as having proclaimed the forgiveness of sins in connection with the inbreaking of the kingdom (see Norman Perrin, *Rediscovering the Teaching of Jesus* [New York: Harper and Row, 1967], pp. 139–40), suggest that this element was part of the original story but that the dispute over the right to forgive sins was a later addition. The view was put forward by Martin Dibelius, *From Tradition to Gospel* (New York: Charles Scribner's Sons, 1965), pp. 44, 66–67. Further on this understanding and the significance of the development of controversy about healings in the traditions, perhaps leading toward an early church interpretation of the reason Jesus was put to death, see A. B. Kolenkow, "Healing Controversy as a Tie Between Miracle and Passion Material for a Proto-Gospel," *JBL* 95 (1976): 623–38. (In this connection one should also notice the strong parallels between Mark 2:1–12 and John 5:1–18. In the Fourth Gospel's story, the immediate controversy is occasioned by Jesus' healing on the Sabbath, although the issue of the man's sin is also mentioned and the question of Jesus' authority is debated. Note again how in John 5:27 the authority to execute judgment is given to Jesus because he is the Son of man.) While the tendency to develop the controversial aspects of the tradition was no doubt strong, one must not overlook the probability that Jesus' words and actions were already controversial in their own time and that the stories may have conveyed overtones and undertones of dispute from their earliest stages.

15. On the literary and rhetorical workings of the story see the several discussions by Dewey in *Markan Public Debate*. Whatever else, she observes, "the style is not clumsy" (p. 76). See also R. T. Mead, "The Healing of the Paralytic—A Unit?" *JBL* 80 (1961): 348–54.

16. In a remarkable number of New Testament stories a sick person is brought by relatives or friends to Jesus or to one of his disciples. Faith, on the part of the friends or the one to be healed, seems to have been of some assistance in many healings. Such faith is frequently although not consistently a factor in the Gospel healing stories. The evangelists appear to have regarded it as an important although not in every instance a necessary ingredient. They describe Jesus' power as such that he could heal without it, although we should not necessarily infer that a lack of reference to faith means it was considered insignificant in a particular story. Of particular interest is the incident reported in Mark 6:1–6 (Matt. 13:53–58) when Jesus can do no mighty works in his home country because of unbelief. It is quite possible that for Jesus himself a willingness to hope in God's ruling power was essential but perhaps all that was essential. See Anton Fridrichsen, *The Problem of Miracle in Primitive Christianity*, trans. Roy A. Harrisville and John S. Hanson (Minneapolis: Augsburg

Publishing House, 1972), pp. 77–84, and Fuller, *Interpreting the Miracles,* pp. 42–45. On the uniqueness and significance of faith in the stories in the Gospel, see Perrin, *Rediscovering the Teaching of Jesus,* pp. 130–43. The theological underpinning for such an understanding is provided by Augustine's teaching that God made us without us but cannot save or justify us without us. See his *Sermons,* CLXIX.11, 13.

With both psychological and spiritual considerations in mind, one must exercise great care, however, in a contemporary ministry of healing not to make the degree of a person's faith the necessary condition for healing. Hope and trust play some role, but to suggest that people can only be healed if they have sufficient faith may add to their anxiety and, if healing does not take place, to a sense of guilt.

17. Austin Farrer is among those who have stressed the anticipation of the resurrection in this narrative, *A Study in Mark* (London: Dacre Press, 1951), p. 47. On controversy leading to Jesus' death see n. 14 above and the discussion of Mark 3:1–6 in chap. 6.

CHAPTER 3

1. What precisely Luke intends by this designation is uncertain. The Greek word is not found elsewhere and may only have been used to emphasize that Zacchaeus was a rich and powerful figure.

2. The Gospels several times link tax collectors with sinners or prostitutes. See Mark 2:15–16; Matt. 11:19; 21:32. Note also the derogatory implications of Matt. 5:46; 18:17. A number of Jewish sources of the time also display this attitude, sometimes speaking of "tax gatherers and robbers" in the same phrase. See J. Jeremias, *Jerusalem in the Time of Jesus: An Investigation into Economic and Social Conditions During the New Testament Period* (Philadelphia: Fortress Press, 1967), pp. 310–12.

3. See Mark 2:14; Luke 5:27–28. In Matt. 9:9 and 10:3 this same figure is called Matthew.

4. On the link between imagination and hope and its vital role in mental health and for religious experience, see W. F. Lynch, *Images of Hope: Imagination as the Healer of the Helpless* (Baltimore: Helicon Press, 1965) and U. T. Holmes, *Ministry and Imagination* (New York: Seabury Press, 1976), esp. pt. 2.

5. Zacchaeus goes far beyond what the law requires; see Lev. 6:5; Num. 5:7; Exod. 22:4, 7; and G. B. Caird, *The Gospel of St. Luke,* Pelican Commentaries (Baltimore: Penguin Books, 1963), p. 208. Note, however, Exod. 22:1.

6. The apparent interjection of considerations of morality is among the reasons why Rudolf Bultmann regards v. 8 as intrusive and a Lukan addition, *The History of the Synoptic Tradition,* trans. John Marsh (New York: Harper and Row, 1963), pp. 33–34. There are various other theories maintaining that v. 9 and/or vv. 8 and 10 were added to the narration to expand upon its meaning. It is interesting, however, that v. 9 (which responds directly to the

challenge of v. 7) speaks of salvation still within the context of the Jewish community.

7. Cf. Norman Perrin, *Rediscovering the Teaching of Jesus* (New York: Harper and Row, 1967), pp. 102–8. Bultmann, *History of the Synoptic Tradition,* p. 34, suggests that the story of Zacchaeus is an imaginary story that was fashioned out of Mark 2:14–17. A number of other scholars, however, find in the story some form of authentic reminiscence coherent with what is otherwise known of Jesus.

8. Jesus may have understood this table fellowship to be an anticipation of the messianic banquet at the end of the age. See Matt. 8:11; Luke 13:29. There, too, the actual guests will not be those who expected to eat with the Messiah. See also Luke 22:25, 30.

9. See P. C. Hodgson, *New Birth of Freedom: A Theology of Bondage and Liberation* (Philadelphia: Fortress Press, 1976), chap. 5, "Jesus the Liberator."

10. There are other passages in the immediate context with comment on Zacchaeus's story. In particular one can compare the story of the rich ruler who was unable to give up his wealth and the subsequent discussion with the disciples about riches and the kingdom of God (Luke 18:18–30). The parable of the pounds or talents immediately follows the Zacchaeus event (Luke 19:11–27). Also, the whole of Luke 16 is concerned with money and wealth, clearly an important subject for the evangelist.

11. "The Son of man came to seek and save the lost" would likely have created an echo with the words describing the ministry of God, the shepherd, in Ezek. 34:16: "I will seek the lost."

12. See Clarence Jordan, *The Cotton Patch Version of Luke and Acts: Jesus' Doings and Happenings* (New York: Association Press, 1969).

13. See especially Luke 10:9; Matt. 10:7–8; Mark 6:7; Luke 9:1; Matt. 10:1; Mark 6:14–15; John 14:12.

14. Jeremias, *Jerusalem in the Time of Jesus,* p. 311, points out that tax collectors could even lose their civil rights because of their profession. By insisting that Zacchaeus too was a son of Abraham, Jesus makes him a full member of the community.

CHAPTER 4

1. For a discussion of ways in which the present story may have been built up from an earlier exorcism narrative, see R. Pesch, "The Markan Version of the Healing of the Gerasene Demoniac," *The Ecumenical Review* 23 (1971): 349–76; and his *Der Besessene von Gerasa,* Stuttgarter Bibelstudien 56 (Stuttgart: KBW, 1972): 41–49. See also J. F. Craghan, "The Gerasene Demoniac," *CBQ* 30 (1968): 522–36. A number of scholars suggest that a basic story may have consisted of something like vv. 2, 7 (8), 11, 14–15. A comparison is often made with the briefer parallel narrative in Mark 1:23–27. The expelling of the demons into the swine may then have come from another story

which was melded with the description of the single exorcism (although several critics hold that some version of the swine story must have been part of the early tale). Other elements were then added through community formation. Vv. 1 and 18–20 are regarded, at least for the most part, as Markan editorial activity. It can be argued, however, that the whole narrative came to Mark virtually in the form in which it is now presented. See P. T. Achtemeier, "Toward the Isolation of Pre-Markan Miracle Catenae," *JBL* 89 (1970): 276; and Rudolf Bultmann, *The History of the Synoptic Tradition*, trans. John Marsh (New York: Harper and Row, 1963), p. 210.

2. One can read the tale as a series of attempts to trick and outsmart the opponent. The theme of an exorcist tricking and even tormenting an evil demon is a common one. See D. E. Nineham, *The Gospel of St. Mark*, Pelican Gospel Commentaries (Baltimore: Penguin Books, 1963), p. 153. The demon knows Jesus' name; then Jesus learns his (or is he given his real name?). Perhaps the demons imagined they were finding safety by passing into the pigs; but they there meet with destruction. On the other hand, the demons might be understood to have outsmarted Jesus for, by so disturbing and destroying the swine, they force him to leave the territory. Yet Jesus does heal the man and leaves him there to tell the story of victory over the demons.

3. Scholars discern the basic pattern of miracle stories in somewhat different ways. See Bultmann, *History of the Synoptic Tradition*, pp. 210, 218–44. Reginald Fuller, *Interpreting the Miracles* (Philadelphia: Westminster Press, 1963), p. 33, is among those who speak of a simpler threefold pattern; e.g., problem, solution, proof of healing. Gerd Theissen, *The Miracle Stories of the Early Christian Tradition*, trans. Francis McDonagh, ed. John Riches (Philadelphia: Fortress Press, 1983), ambitiously analyzes the stories from the perspective of narrative form, historical dimension, and cultural setting and social function. In looking for underlying structure he examines a number of motifs and themes that may be regarded as the structural elements or building blocks for many such narratives. See also R. W. Funk, "The Form of the New Testament Healing Miracle Story" in *Semeia* 12, ed. W. A. Beardslee, *The Poetics of Faith: Essays Offered to Amos Niven Wilder* (Missoula, Mont.: Scholars Press, 1978): 57–96. Funk seeks to develop a "grammar" of component parts and functions that can be applied to all New Testament healing stories.

4. A good parallel to several of the healing stories in the Gospels is an exorcism attributed by Philostratus to Apollonius of Tyana, who lived in the first century A.D. In this case the expelled demon causes a statue to fall down as proof that it has left a previously disturbed young man. *Life of Apollonius* 4:20. See also Josephus, *Jewish Antiquities VIII*, 2:5, in which a fleeing demon is made to overturn a basin of water.

5. While I would argue that this last feature describing some manner of crowd reaction in terms of awe, amazement, fear, or acclamation is part of the fully developed miracle story structure, recent scholarship is correct in pointing out that it is often passed over in the Gospels' narratives. Especially is this true of

Mark, whereas Luke has a pronounced tendency to add it. The issue has taken on importance in the discussion of the manner in which Mark viewed the miracles. Some see him playing down the sensational aspects and even under-cutting the role of Jesus as a wonder worker in order to give stress to an appreciation of Jesus as the one who must suffer. See T. J. Weeden, *Mark: Traditions in Conflict* (Philadelphia: Fortress Press, 1971). D.-A Koch (*Die Bedeutung der Wunderzählungen für die Christologie des Markusevangeliums,* BZNW 22 [Elmsford, N.Y.: Walter De Gruyter, 1975]) makes a special point of citing Mark's frequent *omission* of such acclamations, although it could instead be argued that not all the stories had been given the full form before reaching Mark. If the story of the Gerasene demoniac once circulated in a version that did not include the final verses, it may be noted that v. 15 would have provided a satisfactory ending illustrative of the stage of crowd reaction.

6. The reason for the use of the name Legion is not entirely clear. Perhaps it was a vague reference to indicate the host of forces possessing the man, although a Roman legion at that time would have consisted of more like six thousand soldiers. J. Jeremias, *Jesus' Promise to the Nations,* trans. S. H. Hooke (Phila-delphia: Fortress Press, 1982), pp. 30–31, n. 5, suggests that originally it may merely have meant "soldier" (an attempt to avoid giving the true name?) and that later it was developed into the idea of a large number of demons.

7. This phrase (*ti emoi kai soi*; literally, "what to me and to you?") is harsh and a bit awkward (see Mark 1:24 and 1 Kings 17:18), but would be a fitting kind of stammering effort to ward Jesus off, perhaps by insisting that the realm of evil and Jesus' divine goodness should have nothing to do with one another. Such protective or aversion formulae are found in parallel stories. See Bultmann, *History of the Synoptic Tradition,* p. 209.

8. See Mark 5:41.

9. See Mark 8:22–26; John 9:1–7.

10. This continues in force with respect to much of the rest of the New Testament. Acts (see 3:6, 9:34 with 19:13) suggests that healings were done by the apostles using the name of Jesus Christ of Nazareth. But cf. Acts 19:12.

11. Probably the most notorious example in recent years was *The Exorcist* by W. P. Blatty (New York: Bantam Books, 1971). Note pp. 364–65 where the story of the Gerasene demoniac is read as part of the ritual. In another first-century story (Josephus, *Jewish Antiquities VIII,* 2:5) a ring is placed to a man's nose and the demon drawn out through his nostrils. Not uncommonly such rites were a melange of features drawn from a variety of religious traditions and languages. Practitioners sought by this means to develop a mystique that would convince people of their powers. A highly developed form from a somewhat later period is found in what is known as the Paris Magical Papyrus. It begins:

For those possessed by demons, an approved charm by Pibechis. Take oil made from unripe olives, together with the plant mastigia and lotus pith, and boil it with majoram (very colourless), saying: "Joel, Ossarthiomi,

Emori, Theochipsoith, Sithemeoch, Sothe, Joe, Mimipsothiooph, Phersothi, Aeeioyo, Joe, Eochariphtha: come out of such a one (and the other usual formulae)."

But write this phylactery upon a little sheet of tin: "Jaeo, Abraothioch, Phtha, Mesentiniao, Pheoch, Jaeo, Charsoc," and hang it round the sufferer: it is of every demon a thing to be trembled at, which he fears. Standing opposite, adjure him. The adjuration is this: "I adjure thee by the god of the Hebrews Jesu, Jaba, Jae, Abraoth, Aia, Thoth, Ele, Elo, Aeo, Eu, Jiibaech, Abarmas, Jabarau, Abelbel, Lona, Abra, Maroia, Arm.

The passage continues at some length in this vein. It is translated with a brief introduction and notes by C. K. Barrett in *The New Testament Background: Selected Documents* (New York: Macmillan Co., 1957), pp. 31–35. See his entire section on magical and religious papyri (pp. 29–36). Further, especially on magical and nonmagical emphasis in the synoptic gospels, see J. M. Hull, *Hellenistic Magic and the Synoptic Tradition,* SBT II/28 (Naperville, Ill.: Alec R. Allenson, 1974).

The magical approach to healing represents but one aspect of the diverse approaches of Hellenistic religion and philosophies, which presented many rich psychological and physical as well as more authentically religious insights into the causes of illness and their cures. See Ludwig Edelstein, *Ancient Medicine* (Baltimore: Johns Hopkins Press, 1967).

12. It may be this factor, perhaps together with a desire to show Jesus' dominance over demonic forces, rather than any desire by Mark to develop a secrecy motif with respect to Jesus' messiahship or to downplay his miraculous power, which occasioned the command for silence in stories like 1:23–26; 9:14–29, and 4:36–41. With regard to this second point, see H. C. Kee, *Community of the New Age: Studies in Mark's Gospel* (Philadelphia: Westminster Press, 1977), p. 169, and pp. 165–75 on the secrecy theme in general.

13. This view is also maintained by a number of early theologians. See Lactantius (*The Divine Institutes* 4:15, 9): "And he performed all these things not by his hands, or the application of any remedy, but by his word and commands." So also Lactantius's teacher Arnobius (*Against the Nations* 4:43, 44): "Without any power of incantations, without the juice of herbs and of grasses, without any anxious watching of sacrifices, of libations, of seasons [he did these miracles]." "He wrought without any aid from external things . . . but by the inherent might of his authority."

Hans Dieter Betz is among those who notice how the miraculous event in and of itself is given very little attention in the Christian form of the story. There is a gap in the narrative that represents the awareness that the miracle itself is a divine mystery. See his "The Early Christian Miracle Story: Some Observations on the Form Critical Problem" in *Semeia* 11, ed. R. W. Funk, *Early Christian Miracle Stories* (Missoula, Mont.: Scholars Press, 1978): 69–81.

14. Despite its important place in all three synoptic Gospels, the story is not

found in the three-year cycle of the Roman Catholic Sunday lectionary. In the Sunday lectionary for The Episcopal Church, it occurs only once and then as an optional reading.

15. This may have been among the reasons (more than any specific factors having to do with form or purely historical considerations) that some of the early form-critics were so ready to attribute the story to the activity of the church and to dissociate it from Jesus. See Martin Dibelius, *From Tradition to Gospel* (New York: Charles Scribner's Sons, 1965), p. 292. On the inadequacy of such an approach, see Norman Perrin, *Rediscovering the Teaching of Jesus* (New York: Harper and Row, 1967), pp. 15ff. and 131ff.

16. The French philosopher Paul Ricoeur has contributed greatly to the renaissance of a rehearing of biblical myths and stories through his studies of primary symbols and their relation to narrative contexts. He stresses the importance of a "second naivete" for historically minded, critical twentieth-century individuals who wish to avail themselves of a power and depth of understanding that reaches beyond direct discourse. This form of understanding requires a willingness to hold historical and scientific questions at their own level of significance while attempting to live through the symbols and stories of other times and cultures. See his seminal study, *The Symbolism of Evil* (New York: Harper and Row, 1967), esp. p. 352.

17. One of the several myths of creation popular in the ancient Near East pictured the God forming the world out of the watery chaos depicted as a monster who first had to be defeated and slain. This monster or dragon is given names such as Rahab, Yam, and Leviathan in the Old Testament and other Jewish literature. See Job 9:13; 26:12; Ps. 74:14; 89:10; Isa. 27:1; 30:7; 59:1–10.

18. It was understandably a common belief that gravesites were areas populated by unclean spirits. See H. L. Strack and P. Billerbeck, eds., *Kommentar zum Neuen Testament aus Talmud und Midrasch,* 2d ed. (Munich: C. H. Beck Verlag, 1956), 1:491. On the also-common idea that spiritually dead people dwelt near tombs see Isa. 65:4, a passage that seems to have a curious relationship to this story.

19. See in our chapter 5, the story of the Syrophoenician woman.

20. The area referred to generally as the Decapolis ("the ten cities," v. 20) was a region of, for the most part, newly founded gentile towns stretching to the east and south of Lake Galilee. The extent of Christian activity among them in the first century and afterward is uncertain, but at later dates Christian basilicas were established in several of them.

The evangelists' knowledge of this area seems to have been quite vague. Mark evidently wrote Gerasenes in v. 1. Matthew and a later copyist of Mark's Gospel, recognizing that Gerasa was about thirty miles from Lake Galilee, attempted to correct this to Gadara, six miles away. Other ancient texts indicate different efforts to identify the locale of the story.

21. On "the Most High God" as a gentile way of referring to Israel's God, see Nineham, *The Gospel of St. Mark,* p. 153, and Dan. 3:26; 4:2; Acts 16:17.

22. Not all scholars agree that the theme of mission to the Gentiles was significant in the story, perhaps especially not so in earlier versions. See, however, Pesch, "Markan Version of Healing of Gerasene Demoniac," p. 371; and Nineham, *The Gospel of St. Mark*, p. 151.

23. See Hans Küng, *On Being a Christian*, trans. Edward Quinn (Garden City, N.Y.: Doubleday & Co., 1976), p. 63.

24. This view of Jesus' ministry is emphasized by J. Kallas in *The Significance of the Synoptic Miracles* (London: SPCK, 1961).

25. P. C. Hodgson, *New Birth of Freedom: A Theology of Bondage and Liberation* (Philadelphia: Fortress Press, 1976), p. 42.

26. This is among the lessons to be learned from David Halberstam's study of the key figures involved in the decisions leading to the escalation of warfare in Vietnam, *The Best and the Brightest* (Greenwich, Conn.: Fawcett, 1969).

27. This is one of the vital themes of liberation theology which stresses the need of Christians to recognize the oppressive and demonic forces in themselves and in society, and, through identification with the oppressed, to begin the work of liberation in God's name. See again Hodgson, *New Birth of Freedom*, pp. 208ff.; R. M. Brown, *Theology in a New Key: Responding to Liberation Themes* (Philadelphia: Westminster Press, 1978); and, e.g., Gustavo Gutiérrez, *A Theology of Liberation* (Maryknoll, N.Y.: Orbis Books, 1973), esp. pp. 145–285.

28. From "Holy Baptism," *The Book of Common Prayer* (New York: Church Hymnal Corp., 1979), pp. 302–3.

CHAPTER 5

1. Questions about the language problems Jesus may have encountered in his ministry are entwined with difficult exegetical and historical issues regarding the geographical extent of his ministry. Through this section 7:24—8:26, Mark seems to suggest that Jesus had a rather extended ministry in predominantly gentile areas. Yet the relative lack of Gospel stories dealing with Gentiles, together with sayings like Matt. 10:5–6, 23 and the controversy over the first gentile converts after the resurrection, strongly suggest that Jesus saw his ministry as largely confined if not limited to Jews. (On this issue generally, and with an attempt to interpret it, see J. Jeremias, *Jesus' Promise to the Nations*, trans. S. H. Hooke [Philadelphia: Fortress Press, 1982], esp. pp. 25–39.) Since, however, there were many Jews living in predominantly gentile areas, it could well be that Jesus and his disciples went on forays to what would be regarded as gentile regions. (There is speculation that he did this because he was persecuted or because he was not heeded in his native precincts, but one could just as well argue that he traveled in this manner because of his eagerness to spread the message of the kingdom.)

Our problems in understanding are compounded here by the vagueness of Mark's descriptions. He may be indicating that Jesus went away in the direction of Tyre (Sidon is not included in a number of manuscripts, but see 7:31) and not actually into the coastal area itself. Matthew, by having the woman "come out" from that region in 15:22, seems definitely to indicate that Jesus only went near to gentile territory. P. T. Achtemeier, "Toward the Isolation of Pre-Markan Miracle Catenae" *JBL* 89 (1970): 287, is among those who believe that as originally told the story took place in Galilee rather than on foreign soil (Galilee was well populated with Gentiles), and that it has more consistency on these terms.

Mark's description of the woman as "Greek" means only that she was a non-Jew, a Gentile. That she was a Syrophoenician (distinguishing her from the Libyan Phoenicians) reinforces the fact that she was a pagan. (In his story, Matthew [15:21–28] refers to her still more generally by the older name of Canaanite.) Her first and perhaps only language would then have been Greek, and it is possible that Jesus himself was at least somewhat bilingual. Many of the non-Jews of northern Palestine, especially those of the countryside, had Aramaic for their language, and it is probable that any such encounter would have been conducted in that language. Yet even in the relatively small land area of Palestine there were a number of local dialects and accents. Galilean Aramaic, for instance, could be readily distinguished from the language spoken in Judea; so Peter is recognized in Mark 14:70 (with Matt. 26:73). Probably anyone of the time who traveled some distance from home would have found the language a little different and odd.

2. I have taken the names Justa and Bernice from the retelling and expansion on this story found in the Clementine Homilies (2:19–21; 4:1), which were probably composed in the late second or early third century but dependent in part on somewhat earlier materials.

3. This language of prayer, still in use at some Jewish daily morning services, reaches back to ancient sources. On the distinctly inferior role of women in Judaism at this time, see J. Jeremias, *Jerusalem in the Time of Jesus: An Investigation into Economic and Social Conditions During the New Testament Period* (Philadelphia: Fortress Press, 1967), pp. 359–76. For one evangelist's view of how the disciples would have reacted to Jesus' discussing matters of religion with a woman—in this case a Samaritan woman—see John 4:27. On women in the New Testament generally, see Evelyn Stagg and Frank Stagg, *Women in the World of Jesus* (Philadelphia: Westminster Press, 1978); particularly on the Syrophoenician woman, pp. 113–15.

4. Although the Son of David designation is found in Mark's Bartimaeus story (Mark 10:46–52; see chap. 8, below), and this might indicate an association in his source between the designation and healing, it is Matthew who tends to develop the use of the title in connection with healing using the formula "Have mercy on me, [O Lord,] Son of David." Matt. 9:27; 15:22; 20:30, 31. Since the messianic age would bring healings among its signs (Isa. 35:5–6) and some at least would have seen the Messiah as like a new David, there is good reason for the association. See H. C. Kee, *Community of the New Age: Studies in Mark's Gospel* (Philadelphia: Westminster Press, 1977), pp. 124–29.

5. See the interesting discussion by William Johnston in his chapter "Cosmic

Healing" (esp. p. 132) in *Silent Music: The Science of Meditation* (New York: Harper and Row, 1974).

6. In this sense it has more the feeling of a "pronouncement story" (that is, a story told primarily to point up and preserve an important saying of Jesus) than a healing or miracle narrative, although it has retained its narrative character. See V. Taylor, *The Gospel According to Mark* (London: Macmillan and Co., 1951), p. 347. Achtemeier, "Pre-Markan Miracle Catenae," *JBL* 89 (1970): 287–88, sees the story as the third of five in a second catena of miracle stories taken over from the tradition and used by Mark in his Gospel.

7. Matt. 15:29–31 describes the healing of many people.

8. J. L. McKenzie in *The Jerome Biblical Commentary,* ed. R. E. Brown; J. A. Fitzmyer; R. E. Murphy (Englewood Cliffs, N.J.: Prentice-Hall, 1968), sec. 2, p. 90. McKenzie suggests that Jesus would have been expected to use his wit in keeping with the social and cultural expectations of the time.

9. See again J. Jeremias, *Jesus' Promise to the Nations,* including his bibliography. Reading the narrative of the Syrophoenician woman from a sociological perspective, G. Theissen sees in it evidence of a continuing tension between ethnic groups on the Galilean frontier. The more country-, less city-oriented Jesus movement eventually came to a more liberal attitude as opposed to narrow nationalistic tendencies. *Sociology of Early Palestinian Christianity* (Philadelphia: Fortress Press, 1978), p. 55.

10. See Günther Bornkamm, *Paul* (New York: Harper and Row, 1971), esp. pp. 31–48.

11. Although Luke has probably idealized the struggle over these issues (cf. Paul's words in the heat of battle; Gal. 2:11–16) its lineaments can still be recognized in his report of the "Jerusalem Council" in Acts 15:1–29. It is not clear, however, because of both textual problems and questions of interpretation, whether the so-called apostolic decree issued by the Council (see Acts 15:20, 29; 21:25) was mainly concerned with basic ethical considerations (Gentiles are to aviod idolatry, sexual misbehavior, and murder) or with food laws (Gentiles should not eat anything offered to idols or anything strangled or with blood still in it) or with some combination of the two. See the discussion by B. M. Metzger, *A Textual Commentary on the Greek New Testament* (New York: United Bible Societies, 1971), pp. 429–34. In either case it seems to have been decided that circumcision was not requisite for gentile Christians.

12. See Rom. 1:17; 2:9–10; Acts 13:46; 18:6; 26:20.

13. See Letha Scanzoni and Virginia R. Mollenkott, *Is the Homosexual My Neighbor? Another Christian View* (San Francisco: Harper and Row, 1978).

14. See Acts 10—11:8, but also with Gal. 2:11–16.

CHAPTER 6

1. This paragraph is taken from the Babylonian Talmud, Kiddušhin 30b.

2. An illustration of how stories like these continued to be retold and sometimes elaborated upon in early Christian lore was to be found, according to Jerome, in the gospel of the Nazaraeans: "the man who had a withered hand is

described as a mason who pleaded for help in the following words: I was a mason and earned [my] livelihood with [my] hands; I beseech thee, Jesus, to restore me to health that I may not with ignominy have to beg for my bread." Jerome, *Commentary on Matthew*, on Matt. 12:13. See *New Testament Apocrypha*, vol. 1, ed. R. McL. Wilson, from the German edition ed. W. Schneemelcher (Philadelphia: Westminster Press, 1963) p. 148. Luke 6:6 tells us it was the man's right hand.

3. See Mark 10:6–9; Matt. 19:4–8 with Gen. 2:24. In this passage, too, Jesus seems to go beyond the letter of the law, or even any conservative or liberal interpretation of it, to a more radical understanding based on its true purpose. On the Jewish teachings, see V. Taylor, *The Gospel According to Mark* (London: Macmillan and Co., 1951), pp. 417–18, with his references to other literature.

4. The ancient Jewish Kaddish prayer contained this petition: "May he let his kingdom rule in your lifetime and in your days and in the lifetime of the whole house of Israel, speedily and soon." See J. Jeremias, *The Prayers of Jesus*, SBT 2, no. 2 (Naperville, Ill.: Alec R. Allenson, 1967): 98.

5. Typical of several rabbinic-style statements, like Yakim's prayer, is the saying from the later commentary on Leviticus *Sifra* 93d: "He who is separated from iniquity receives to himself the kingdom of God."

6. See Jer. 31:31–34.

7. Mark 7:9–13.

8. Mark 2:23–28; Matt. 12:1–8; Luke 6:1–5. This story immediately precedes the story of the man with the withered hand.

9. Jesus' question is found in Matthew's version of the story, 12:11–12. See also Luke 13:15–16 and 14:5.

10. For examples from the later Jewish codification of the oral traditions, see C. K. Barrett, *The New Testament Background: Selected Documents* (New York: Macmillan Co., 1957), pp. 153–55. While these rabbinic writings are products of a Judaism that took shape after the death of Jesus and the later fall of Jerusalem in A.D. 70 and cannot casually be used to illustrate Jewish attitudes before that time, it is clear from a critical study of the New Testament and other historical sources that the basis of many of the viewpoints in these writings (and in some cases the actual sayings) reach back to the time of Jesus and before.

11. The Damascus Document CD 11:13–14. See this whole section, 10:14—11:18, on sabbath regulations.

12. The Mishnah tractate *Shabbath* 18:3. This tractate, which debates and discusses a myriad of sabbath regulations, often in extensive detail, can be found in the translation by Herbert Danby, *The Mishnah* (London: Oxford University Press, 1933), pp. 100–121.

13. Mishnah tractate *Yoma* 8:6. On the Jewish tradition that the sabbath regulations could be violated only to save a life, see E. Lohse, "Jesu Worte über den Sabbat," in *Judentum, Urchristentum, Kirche: Festschrift für Joachim Jeremias*, ed. W. Eltester, BZNW 26 (Berlin: Töpelmann, 1960): 79–89.

14. A. C. Wire ("The Structure of the Gospel Miracle Stories and Their Tellers" in *Semeia* 11, ed. R. W. Funk [1978]: 83–113; see also pp. 93–94)

gives examples of rabbinical stories in which there is a struggle between those who defend a strict construction of the law and those who would break through the law's restrictions—the latter group then being supported by some manner of miracle, usually the hearing of a divine voice.

15. Mark 2:27. The "they" of 3:2 seems to refer in a stylized manner to the same audience of Jesus' opponents found in 2:23–28.

16. *Mekilta* on Exod. 31:13 (109b).

17. See Matt. 9:13; 12:7.

18. In *Homily VII*, on St. John, sec. 8.

19. See Rom. 13:1–7; Tit. 3:1; 1 Pet. 2:13–14. This attitude can in some measure be explained by the need of the small Christian communities, often regarded as a foreign and perhaps subversive element in the societies of the Roman Empire, to be viewed as a lawful religion, not threatening to the legitimate powers of the state and thus safe from persecution.

20. A still more traditional form for debate would be "Is it lawful to do such and such a good act on the sabbath?" We note again that John 5:2–18 presents this Gospel's version of the healing of a paralyzed man (cf. Mark 2:1–12) as a sabbath healing controversy. The justification for Jesus' activity on the sabbath is given in 5:17: "My father is working still, and I am working." While Old Testament tradition would indicate (see Num. 15:32–36) that one might be put to death for carrying a bed (or perhaps ordering a similar action) on the sabbath, it is far from certain that the mere act of stretching out a hand would have been regarded as a sabbath violation. The fact that Jesus does not touch the man might also suggest that he was attempting to heal within the context of a strict interpretation of sabbath law. The Markan story, however, does not seem concerned with such considerations.

21. See D. O. Via, Jr., *Kerygma and Comedy in the New Testament: A Structuralist Approach to Hermeneutic* (Philadelphia: Fortress Press, 1975), p. 132.

22. Note also Matt. 22:15; John 11:53.

23. See chap. 2, n. 14.

24. The ironic manner in which controversy over healing and saving acts leads to Jesus' death, which will then bring his new life and new healing and life to others, is presented still more forcefully in the Fourth Gospel where the raising of Lazarus to new life becomes the catalyst for Jesus' death. Recall how Anitra Kolenkow (*JBL* 95 [1976]: 623–38) finds this pattern of healing leading to controversy pointing to suffering already part of the experience of the early church.

25. Reginald Fuller (*Interpreting the Miracles* [Philadelphia: Westminster Press, 1963], pp. 51–52) points to the messianic connotations of "to do good" and "to save life." For an interpretation of eschatology and "end time" in Jesus' message, see F. H. Borsch, *God's Parable* (Philadelphia: Westminster Press, 1975), pp. 27–44.

26. G. S. Sloyan in *Is Christ the End of the Law?* (Philadelphia: Westminster Press, 1978) argues that Jesus intended that the just demands of the law must be kept. Matthew's Gospel presents Jesus as the true interpreter of the law, not

contrasting grace and law but showing how the way of love enables the law's fulfillment (see pp. 49–56; on the not dissimilar presentations of the other synoptic evangelists more generally, see pp. 38–69). In a more detailed, redactional study, *Jesus and the Law in the Synoptic Tradition,* SNTSMS 28 (Cambridge: Cambridge University Press, 1975), Robert Banks finds that Jesus' ministry presented a more radical challenge to both the Jewish oral tradition, which had grown up as a way of actually subverting the genuine requirements of the law, and to any attitude toward the law that set it above the demands of the kingdom.

27. On Paul's personal understanding of the role of the law in his life, see the whole of Romans 7, and then more generally Romans 1—4 with Galatians 3—5. For one explication of Paul's view together with bibliographical notes, see Sloyan, *Is Christ the End of the Law?,* pp. 70–106. See also V. P. Furnish, *Theology and Ethics in Paul* (Nashville: Abingdon Press, 1968), pp. 135–62.

28. On the alienating power of the law and the Spirit of Jesus in the traditions as a catalyst for new freedom, see P. C. Hodgson, *New Birth of Freedom: A Theology of Bondage and Liberation* (Philadelphia: Fortress Press, 1976), pp. 187–90; 233–35; 312–21.

29. On the new authority in these words of Jesus which set his teachings above rabbinic interpretations of the law, see Ernst Käsemann, *Essays on New Testament Themes,* trans. W. J. Montague (Philadelphia: Fortress Press, 1982), pp. 37–38.

30. So Mark 2:21–22 which is at the center of the 2:1—3:6 cycle.

31. See D. E. Nineham, *The Gospel of St. Mark,* Pelican Gospel Commentaries (Baltimore: Penguin Books, 1963), p. 111. In 6:52 and 8:17 Mark uses similar phraseology to describe the disciples' response to Jesus. People of the time generally regarded the heart as the seat of the intellect. It is here the understanding more than the emotions that is blinded.

32. Mark's mention of the Herodians along with the Pharisees (see also Mark 12:13 and perhaps 8:15) continues to be somewhat of a puzzle to scholars. Matthew and Luke either partially or totally avoid the designation. In no other literature do we find a group called Herodians. It may be that Mark only intended a general reference to those who aligned themselves with the political prerogatives and aspirations of Herod Antipas, or still more generally with local political rule in Palestine claiming a legitimacy from the first King Herod.

33. On Albert Schweitzer's understanding of Jesus' interim or conditional ethic, see *The Mystery of the Kingdom of God: The Secret of Jesus' Messiahship and Passion* (New York: Dodd, Mead, 1914), pp. 99–105.

CHAPTER 7

1. There are enough dissimilarities between the Markan passage (where Jesus first presents the double commandment) and Luke's version of the dialogue to suggest that their versions could have had separate origins. Jeremias thinks that Jesus may have been involved in such a discussion on more than one

occasion. See *The Parables of Jesus,* rev. ed. (New York: Charles Scribner's Sons, 1963), p. 202. Most scholars, however, posit one basic story, holding that, while Luke knew Mark's version (he omits it at the corresponding point in his own Gospel), there are enough similarities between Luke and Matthew (e.g., the man is said to be "testing" Jesus, whom he addresses as "Teacher") as to indicate another source for a slightly different version of the original story.

Is Luke or Matthew more faithful to that version? It has long been suggested that Luke presents it more faithfully, especially in that he has the lawyer rather than Jesus recite the love commandment. In recent years, however, it has been argued that this, along with his casting the whole issue in terms of a more universalistic question about eternal life, may be a sign of Luke's editorial activity. This form of question would better suit a gentile audience, and the recitation of the double commandment by the lawyer could have been borrowed from the second part of Mark's version in order better to lead into the lawyer's next question and thus provide the link to the parable.

2. J. D. Crossan holds that Luke 10:25–28 (the question about eternal life and the lawyer's response) and the original parable (10:30–35 only) were distinct units woven together with the editorial aid of 10:29 and vv. 36–37. Crossan especially notes the different uses of "neighbor" in 10:27, 29 and 10:36 where first it is employed passively (of one to whom mercy is offered) and then actively (of one who offers mercy). Contrary to most other scholars who hold for two discrete units which Luke first joined together, Crossan suggests that this had already been accomplished in Q and that Matthew omitted the parable, especially because of its making a hero of a Samaritan (see Matt. 10:5). See Crossan's "Parable and Example in the Teaching of Jesus," *NTS* 18 (1971–73): 285–307; and *In Parables: The Challenge of the Historical Jesus* (New York: Harper and Row, 1973) pp. 57–66. Another view is presented by Eta Linnemann who holds that 10:29–37 may once have existed as a separate unit to which 10:25–28 was later added, "neighbor" being the link word. See her *Jesus of the Parables* (New York: Harper and Row, 1966), p. 202.

3. See particularly R. W. Funk, *Language, Hermeneutic and Word of God* (New York: Harper and Row, 1966), pp. 199–222.

4. In the literature of Judaism and many other cultures it is part of a well-known story form to have two figures act in one way and then to have a third character act in a contrasting manner. The fact that the first two men are associated with the practice of religion has led to speculation that some earlier version of the story may have contrasted the response of a Jewish layman to that of the priest and Levite. See Jeremias, *Parables,* p. 204.

5. Crossan rightly observes that Luke 10:34–35 so stresses the goodness of the Samaritan that no reader or hearer could question it. What the parable surprisingly—even shockingly—does is to put two terms into an equation many hearers would have regarded as impossible: Samaritan = good.

Because of Luke's special interest in Samaria and Samaritans (Luke 9:52; 17:11, 16 esp., and Acts 1:8; 8:1 ff.; 9:31; 15:3), there has long been a suspicion that Luke himself may have so designated the stranger. This possibility should be seen in the light of Christianity's early missionary ventures in Samaria (as described in Acts) but also with the hints in the Fourth Gospel regarding Jesus' own links with Samaria: see John 4:4 ff. and especially the implications of John 4:44 and 8:48.

6. Jeremias, *Parables*, p. 204, suggests that the traveler would have been a merchant.

7. Following Eberhard Jüngel, Norman Perrin wondered if the rabbinic teaching that to accept an act of almsgiving or help from a Samaritan would mean to delay the redemption of Israel might have passed through the injured man's mind or that of a Jewish hearer of the parable. *Jesus and the Language of the Kingdom: Symbol and Metaphor in New Testament Interpretation* (Philadelphia: Fortress Press, 1976), p. 119.

8. "The future that the parable discloses is the future of every hearer who grasps and is grasped by his position in the ditch." Funk in *Language, Hermeneutic and Word of God*, p. 214. Funk is among those who stress the secular, everyday character of Jesus' parables as descriptive of the world where human destiny is at stake. Here is where God's action happens, and the logic of everydayness is broken into by unexpected turns that cause one to see through the commonplace to a new reality.

9. Crossan in "Parable and Example in the Teaching of Jesus," *NTS* 18 (1971–72): 295. This essay is also included in *Semeia 1: A Structuralist Approach to the Parables*, ed. R. W. Funk (Missoula, Mont.: Scholars Press, 1974), which explores the form and function of parables. On the function and force of parable as metaphor as distinguished from allegory and exemplary story, see Perrin, *Jesus and the Language of the Kingdom*, pp. 89–193. In this discussion Perrin focuses particularly on the parable of the good Samaritan and summarizes recent research. See also *Semeia 2: The Good Samaritan*, ed. J. D. Crossan (Missoula, Mont.: Scholars Press, 1974).

10. Crossan rightly points out that, whatever the history of the story's composition, discourse and parable are now woven together by the twice-repeated pattern of (*a*) the lawyer's question, (*b*) Jesus' responding question (in the second instance consisting largely of the parable itself), (*c*) the lawyer's answer, (*d*) Jesus' exhortation. I am also suggesting that the different uses of the word *neighbor* (Who is one to be neighbor to? Who acts as neighbor?), rather than only conflicting with one another as they do on the surface of the passage, are subtly employed at a deeper structural level to help the lawyer perceive his real question and also, at this level, to integrate the discourse and parable. At this level, too, the parable can function as true parable rather than as exemplary story.

11. The word for "to test" (*ek-peirazō*) has connotations of "to tempt." On several occasions Jesus is said to have been so tested by his opponents, first by the devil. See Luke 4:2, 12.

12. The question is closely paralleled in Luke 18:18; Mark 10:17/Matt. 19:16—the story of the rich young man. Luke may have borrowed the question from that context or there could be a more complex relationship with that

story which continues on to present the commandments about regard for one's neighbor.

13. The double commandment is formed by a combination of Deut. 6:5 and Lev. 19:18. There is considerable debate about whether this summary already existed in Jewish teaching of the time. G. Bornkamm holds that any such summary would have been contrary to a rabbinic attitude toward the law. "Das Dopplegebot der Liebe," in W. Eltester, ed., *Neutestamentliche Studien für Rudolf Bultmann;* BZNW 21 (Berlin: Töpelmann, 1954), pp. 85–93, esp. p. 86. On a comparison of the synoptic versions and a discussion of its origins, see R. H. Fuller, "The Double Commandment of Love: A Test Case for the Criteria of Authenticity," in *Essays on the Love Commandment,* ed. R. H. Fuller (Philadelphia: Fortress Press, 1978), pp. 41–56. Versions of such a double commandment are found in *The Testament of the Twelve Patriarchs* (Dan. 5:3; Issachar 5:2; 7:6) which likely originated in Judaism. The commandment to love one's neighbor, seen as a kind of summary of the law, plays an important role in early Christian teaching. See Matt. 19:19; Rom. 13:8–10; Gal. 5:14; Jas. 2:8. See also Matt. 7:12.

14. See Num. 21:1–3. Jeremias (*Parables,* p. 204) rightly points out, however, that this restriction would not technically have applied to the Levite.

15. For a detailed report of the experiment, including the study of other variables, such as personality tests and the fact that some of the subjects were asked to be prepared to give a talk on the parable of the good Samaritan (!), see John M. Darley and C. Daniel Batson, "From Jerusalem to Jericho: A Study of Situational and Dispositional Variables in Helping Behavior," *Journal of Personality and Social Psychology* 27 (1973): 100–108. More disquieting studies have indicated that it may be especially those who insist on "law and order," who are bent more on punishing the perpetrators than helping the victims of a crime, who have the strongest tendency to intervene in so-called good Samaritan situations. See "The Angry Samaritans," *Psychology Today* (June 1976): 61.

16. We agree with Crossan that, if the original story had been primarily intended as an illustration and exemplification of Jesus' imperative to love enemies, then, for a Jewish audience, the injured man should have been a Samaritan. But true parables, like many a good story, are often rich with additional allusions that extend out from the central metaphorical movement of the narrative.

17. In the larger context of this passage Jesus has begun the long trip to Jerusalem, which will end with his taking the road up from Jericho to his passion. In this way he will be a healer to many whom he meets.

A general theme that might be used for the section Luke 9:51—11:13 is "the meaning of discipleship." So G. B. Caird, *The Gospel of St. Luke,* Pelican Gospel Commentaries (Baltimore: Penguin Books, 1963), pp. 139–53. Luke clearly intends the discourse and parable to be instructive for all who would follow Jesus, and the story gives content to the mission (see esp. 10:9) that is presented earlier in the chapter. A relationship can also be drawn with the subsequent story of Martha and her sister Mary. The anxious concern of Martha might be paralleled with the lawyer's need to justify himself and contrasted with the unassuming charity of the Samaritan.

CHAPTER 8

1. Paul Ricoeur speaks of the process of reorientation by disorientation as one of the strategies of biblical language. See "Biblical Hermeneutics," in *Semeia* 4, ed. J. D. Crossan (1975): 71.

2. R. H. Fuller describes the story as a coda in *Preaching the New Lectionary* (Collegeville, Minn.: The Liturgical Press, 1974), p. 441. Many scholars emphasize the crucial placement of the Bartimaeus story; see P. J. Achtemeier, "'And He Followed Him': Miracles and Discipleship in Mark 10:46–52," in *Semeia* 11, ed. R. W. Funk (1978): 115–45.

3. On Mark's often negative portrayal of the disciples as a foil for true discipleship, see W. H. Kelber, *Mark's Story of Jesus* (Philadelphia: Fortress Press, 1979), esp. chaps. 2 and 3.

4. Matthew makes the comparison stronger still by having two blind men healed, Matt. 20:29–34. Matthew has a close parallel to the Bartimaeus story in 9:27–31. It may be that there were a number of stories in circulation of Jesus' healing blind persons, although Matthew could have formulated 9:27–31 out of Mark 10:46–52 and 8:22–26.

5. The *en tē hodō* of Mark 10:32 and 46 form an obvious *inclusio*, helping us to see the included material as a whole and to draw the appropriate parallels and contrasts. "The way" in later New Testament piety (particularly in Acts) becomes virtually synonymous with Christian faith. It begins to have this nuance in Mark 1:2, 3; 6:8; 8:27; 9:33, 34; 10:17.

Mark 10:32–34 is the third of the formal passion predictions in Mark's Gospel; the others are 8:31 and 9:31–32. Here as elsewhere Mark notes the fear of Jesus' followers which he associates with their inability fully to comprehend Jesus and his mission.

6. The opening of Mark's story is seemingly awkward, especially with its double mention of Jericho and the manner in which the disciples and the crowd are included in the scene. It is possible that one of Mark's reasons for placing the story at this juncture is that the tradition already contained a reference to Jericho. Since Mark wished to have Bartimaeus follow Jesus "on the way," he had to move the setting to Jesus' exit from the city. It was, of course, also important to stress that the disciples were present to witness the event.

7. Although it has long been maintained that the traditions tend to add details such as personal names to the narratives, it has become increasingly evident that there is no fixed rule in this regard. Both Matthew and Luke, presumably writing after Mark and making use of his version, do not include the name. Many scholars believe the name Bartimaeus was already present in the tradition, perhaps reaching back to a reminiscence concerning an early disciple of Jesus, possibly from Jericho. The Greek explanation of his name

("son of Timaeus"; the Aramaic would have been "Timai") may have arisen in the Greek-speaking community before Mark incorporated the narrative into his Gospel. See E. S. Johnson, Jr., "Mark 10:46–52: Blind Bartimaeus," *CBQ* 40 (1978): 191–204, esp. 193.

8. On the number of beggars in Jerusalem see Jeremias, *Jerusalem in the Time of Jesus: An Investigation into Economic and Social Conditions During the New Testament Period* (Philadelphia: Fortress Press, 1967), pp. 116–18.

9. Mark four times makes reference to David in his Gospel, in this story, at 2:25, 11:10 and 12:35–37. There is considerable debate about whether Mark intends to give a positive value to the title in 12:35–37. Also on the title, see chap. 5, n. 4.

We are probably meant to perceive some form of progression from the more general designation of Jesus as the one from Nazareth in v. 47 to the honorific if ambiguous and dangerous Son of David to the more personal and intimate *rabbounei,* "my master" or "teacher."

10. Critics differ on their understanding of the background of the story. V. K. Robbins ("The Healing of Blind Bartimaeus [10:46–52] in Markan Theology," *JBL* 92 [1973]: 224–43) is among those who believe we are dealing with what was originally a brief healing narrative which Mark has heavily rewritten in order to develop the picture of Bartimaeus as the type of true disciple and to lead into the story of Jesus' entrance into Jerusalem and the passion. Achtemeier, on the other hand (in "And He Followed Him," in *Semeia* 11), holds that Mark has taken over an already developed tradition about discipleship in which the healing miracle was of secondary significance. Mark, he maintains, both understood and used the developed tradition as a call-to-discipleship story since the evangelist does not see a positive relationship between miracle and coming to faith in Jesus.

On the basis of these differing understandings it is not surprising that there is no agreement with regard to the form of the story. Dieter Betz is probably right to speak of it as a mixed form—both a miracle and a conversion story, with the conclusion revealing the primary thrust of the narrative. See his "The Early Christian Miracle Story: Some Observations on the Form Critical Problem," in *Semeia* 11, ed. R. H. Funk (1978): 69–81, where he also offers a detailed outline of the narrative elements of the story.

11. On *akolouthein* as an allusion to discipleship in Mark see 1:18; 2:14, 15; 6:1; 9:38; 10:28; 15:41; and esp. 8:34; 10:21, 32 with reference to following Jesus to the cross.

12. See esp. Phil. 3:4–11.

13. *The Dark Night of the Soul,* 2:2, 5 in *The Complete Works of St. John,* vol. 1, trans. E. A. Peers, rev. ed. (London: Burns, Oates and Washbourne, 1953).

14. Prologue to *The Ascent of Mt. Carmel,* trans. Peers, vol. 1, sec. 4.

15. See the discussion by Kenneth Leech of the number of theologians and mystics who recognize that "the dark night represents a theological reality, not simply a transitory human experience of forsakedness. It is an essential element

of revelation." *Soul Friend: The Practice of Christian Spirituality* (New York: Harper and Row, 1980), pp. 159–64; quotation from p. 163.

16. See *Summa Theologica* I, I, 20 article 2; and II, II, 66 article 6.

17. *The Cloud of Unknowing,* chap. 4. In the translation by Clifton Walters, *The Cloud of Unknowing and Other Works* (New York: Penguin Books, 1978), p. 63.

18. T. S. Eliot in *The Four Quartets,* part III of "East Coker." *The Complete Poems and Plays, 1909–1950.* (New York: Harcourt Brace Jovanovich, 1952), pp. 126–27.

19. The Bartimaeus story is probably meant to intimate the mysterious interrelationship between the Lord's initiative along with the gift character of love and the role of the disciple's readiness and faith. See my discussion in chap. 2, n. 16, on the roles of hope and faith in healing situations.

20. The Prologue to *The Ascent of Mt. Carmel,* vol. 1, section 1.

CHAPTER 9

1. For a survey of some of the interpretations of the Corinthians' behavior and beliefs, see C. K. Barrett, *A Commentary on the Second Epistle to the Corinthians* (New York: Harper and Row, 1973), pp. 28–30, and at various points in his notes. More generally and on the apostle's life and theology, see Günther Bornkamm, *Paul* (New York: Harper and Row, 1971).

2. For the view that the superlative apostles were exponents of an already developed Jewish-gnostic movement, see Walter Schmithals, *Gnosticism in Corinth: An Investigation of the Letters to the Corinthians* (Nashville: Abingdon Press, 1971). Dieter Georgi, however, sees Paul's opponents as Hellenistic Jewish missionaries from Palestine who have been influenced by the ideas and methods of the wandering philosophical prophets and miracle workers of the Hellenistic world. They view themselves as supermen who have risen above the ordinary mortal condition and have the power to confer like status upon their followers. Such missionaries would establish their authority by their power to work miracles and wonders. See his *Die Gegner des Paulus im 2 Korintherbrief* (Neukirchen-Vluyn: Neukirchen, 1964). In his article, "Eine Christus-Aretalogie bei Paulus (2 Kor. 12, 7–10)" *ZTK* 66 (1969): 288–305, H. D. Betz finds evidence that Paul's opponents saw themselves as miracle and wonder workers. In the face of their claims, Paul presents his own healing story, in form, like many another healing-miracle story of the era, except that God denies the healing requested and shows Paul a different kind of power in association with the crucified one.

3. See 2 Cor. 10:2 where Paul claims not to be acting in this fashion.

4. For a brief discussion of the variety of explanations (including the possibility that the thorn was his inability to convert the Jews to the gospel) see C. K. Barrett, *Second Epistle to the Corinthians,* pp. 314–15. For the view that Paul was troubled by neuralgic pains, see J. Lindblom, *The Bible: A Modern Understanding* (Philadelphia: Fortress Press, 1973), p. 181.

5. See also Rom. 16:22; 1 Cor. 16:21; Philemon 19: Col. 4:18; 2 Thess. 3:17. Although the last two letters are thought by some to have been written by disciples, they could yet reflect an authentic reminiscence.

6. Paul's own memory of his calling may be alluded to in 2 Cor. 12:2–4. If he is referring there to the same experience described in Acts, then Acts has apparently considerably objectified what was to Paul an encounter difficult to describe.

7. Krister Stendahl offers a helpful corrective to views of Paul's calling which too easily apply later church understanding of conversion or introspective psychological interpretations to the apostle's words. See his *Paul Among Jews and Gentiles and Other Essays* (Philadelphia: Fortress Press, 1976), pp. 7–23.

8. On the cross as God's signature, see E. Käsemann, *Perspectives on Paul,* trans. Margaret Kohl (Philadelphia: Fortress Press, 1971), p. 56. It is the thesis of Jürgen Moltmann's *The Crucified God: The Cross of Christ as the Foundation and Criticism of Christian Theology* (New York: Harper and Row, 1974) that with the death of Jesus either the concept of God had to be abandoned or God be seen as a crucified God.

9. For a developed discussion of this theme, see David Ray Griffin, /*God, Power and Evil: A Process Theodicy* (Philadelphia: Westminster Press, 1976). Moltmann writes, "God in Auschwitz and Auschwitz in the crucified God— that is the basis for a real hope which both embraces and overcomes the world, and the ground for a love which is stronger than death and can sustain death. It is the ground for living with the terror of history and the end of history, and nevertheless remaining in love and meeting what comes in openness for God's future. It is the ground for living and bearing guilt and sorrow for the future of man in God." *The Crucified God,* p. 278.

10. A number of scholars believe that there is evidence in the New Testament that some early Christians portrayed and worshiped Jesus as a kind of divine-hero man. They emphasized Jesus' miraculous powers (along with those of his followers) to the point that distinctions between the historical Jesus and the risen Lord began to blur in such a way that any real understanding of the historical Jesus' humanity and suffering was lost or strongly minimized. In his study of Mark, T. J. Weeden argues that this evangelist wrote his Gospel largely in order to combat and correct such a view of Jesus, adding a passion narrative to already extant cycles of miracle stories and presenting Jesus as the Son of man who must suffer before his resurrection. See *Mark: Traditions in Conflict* (Philadelphia: Fortress Press, 1971), esp. pp. 52–69. This view of Jesus which Mark is attacking would correspond with the Christology of Paul's opponents in Corinth, as interpreted by Dieter Georgi (see n. 2 above), which Paul also had to find ways to controvert. See also P. J. Achtemeier, "The Origin and Function of the Pre-Markan Miracle Catenae," *JBL* 91 (1972): 209–12.

11. Ernst Keller and Marie-Luise Keller, *Miracles in Dispute: A Continuing Debate* (Philadelphia: Fortress Press, 1969), p. 187, point out that many in Corinth, as many today, had trouble hearing Paul's presentation of the gospel, not because of miracles, but because they could not accept a crucified Lord.

12. The problem of suffering and evil has posed grave difficulties for most religions. How can God at the same time be the almighty one and also good while yet there is so much inexplicable wrong and pain in the world? Attempts to fashion a theodicy (a justification of God's ways and purposes) have usually not questioned God's goodness but have either tried to deny the existence of true evil or to qualify or interpret in some manner God's omnipotence. See John Bowker, *Problems of Suffering in Religions of the World* (Cambridge: Cambridge University Press, 1970); John Hick, *Evil and the God of Love* (London: Macmillan and Co., 1966) and Griffin, *God, Power and Evil.* Especially with respect to the biblical perspective, see W. S. Towner, *How God Deals with Evil* (Philadelphia: Westminster Press, 1976). For a powerful contemporary reflection, see Dorothee Soelle, *Suffering,* trans. Everett Kalin (Philadelphia: Fortress Press, 1975).

13. On the theme of Paul experiencing suffering because of his apostolic ministry and so showing forth in his life the suffering of the earthly Jesus recognized to be the same Jesus as the exalted Lord, see Erhardt Güttgemanns, *Die leidende Apostel und sein Herr: Studien zur paulinischen Christologie* (Göttingen: Vandenhoeck and Ruprecht, 1966). The apostle discovers the authenticity of his ministry, not in spiritual experience or even his commissioning, but in the measure that his life and teaching reflect that of the crucified Jesus. See also E. Käsemann, "Die Legitimität des Apostels," *ZNTW* 41 (1942): 33–71.

14. *Letters and Papers from Prison,* enlarged ed. (New York: Macmillan Co., 1971), p. 361. See also Rom. 8:17; 1 Pet. 4:13–14.

15. See Soelle, *Suffering,* pp. 162–78.

16. Note also Bonhoeffer in *Letters and Papers from Prison,* p. 391.

17. See also Rom. 15:19; Gal. 3:5; and the references to the working of miracles in 1 Cor. 12:10, 28–29.

18. See Moltmann, *The Crucified God,* esp. pp. 219–27.

19. Again, see the study of the rise of scientific and historic consciousness in Keller and Keller, *Miracles in Dispute.* Note particularly (pp. 159–80) their doubts that the insights of quantum mechanics and especially the principle of indeterminacy should be used as a way of making room for divine miracles.

20. See pp. 59–60.

21. On this awareness see Käsemann, *Perspectives on Paul,* p. 153.

22. For this description of Paul's opponents see Stendahl, *Paul Among Jews and Gentiles,* p. 46.

23. It is not difficult to see how this might have happened since someone collecting the correspondence, perhaps twenty or thirty years after the letters were written, would very likely have been uncertain about the interconnection of the various materials, parts of which may also have become detached from their original context. On the several possibilities and their ramifications, and with reference to the views of those who maintain the integrity of 1 and 2 Corinthians, see Barrett, *Second Epistle to the Corinthians,* pp. 5–20. Most important for our purposes is the possibility that 2 Cor. 10—13 was

originally a separate letter written before 2 Cor. 1—9. Chaps. 10—13 could then be the so-called painful letter mentioned in 2 Cor. 2:4–11; 7:8–12 (although 7:12 may refer back to the incident of 1 Cor. 5:1–5). Several statements in 2 Corinthians 1—9 seem to presuppose or echo language used in chaps. 10—13; e.g., 1:23 with 13:2, 2:3 with 13:10, and 2:9 with 10:6. Although this theory does not satisfactorily answer all questions raised by a careful study of the extant letters (quite possibly more letters were written than have survived), it does seem to make the best sense to see 2 Corinthians 1—9 (or at least 1:1—6:13 and 7:2–16) as the conciliatory letter written after the painful epistolary confrontation of 10—13. Barrett, however, favors a theory in which the painful letter referred to in 2 Cor. 2:4 is missing and chaps. 10—13 are a sequel to 1—9, written after news had reached Paul that the embassy of Titus bearing 2 Corinthians 1—9 met with failure and further criticism of Paul.

24. Again the sequence of events is difficult to establish with any certainty. After Paul's original stay in Corinth he went to Ephesus. Paul seems to have originally planned to return from Ephesus passing through Macedonia to Corinth (see 1 Cor. 16:1–5 with 4:19–20). He then, however, changed his mind, intending to give the Corinthians the pleasure of a double visit (2 Cor. 1:15–16), coming to Corinth first, then going to Macedonia, afterwards returning to Corinth. But the first of these return visits turned out to be somewhat of a disaster. Hurt and irate, Paul returned by way of Macedonia to Ephesus, where—while apparently also troubled by illness—he wrote his angry and painful letter. His failure to return to Corinth seems to have occasioned further criticisms of him as fickle and indecisive (2 Cor. 1:17–23). Titus was sent as the bearer of this letter (2 Corinthians 10—13). Now Paul, unable to wait in Ephesus, himself set out for Troas and then Macedonia where Titus met him with the good news of the change in heart on the part of the Corinthians. Paul then made his third visit to Corinth (see 2 Cor. 12:14; 13:1).

25. A helpful exposition with illustrations of this insight is presented by Henri Nouwen, *The Wounded Healer* (Garden City, N.Y.: Doubleday and Co., 1972).

26. See Acts 15:36–40, but also Col. 4:10.

27. See Gal. 2:11–16.

28. See 1 Clem. 1:1; 3; 46:9; 47:5–7. Clement's letter was an official communication from the church in Rome occasioned by a dispute created when younger members of the church in Corinth deposed certain elders from the ministry.

29. See 2 Cor. 12:20–21.